Quick Guid[e for] Managers

Quick Guide #3

Strategic Benchmarking: Beyond Numbers

Michel Theriault

WoodStone Press
Toronto, Canada

Published 2018 by WoodStone Press

Print Edition   ISBN 978-0-9937733-2-7

epub Edition   ISBN 978-0-9937733-3-4

Kindle Edition ISBN 978-0-9937733-4-1

Table of Contents

INTRODUCTION 7

  BENCHMARKING IS A STRATEGIC TOOL 9

    Benefits of Benchmarking 10

  USING THIS BOOK 11

    Section 1 - Foundations of Benchmarking 12

    Section 2 - Conducting Benchmarking 12

    Section 3 - Implementing Change 13

SECTION 1 –FOUNDATIONS OF BENCHMARKING 15

    Benchmarking For Results 16

    Why Benchmark? 18

    What is Benchmarking Not? 21

    Traditional versus Strategic Benchmarking 22

    Your Benchmarking Plan – Your Experience 25

  PREREQUISITES FOR BENCHMARKING 26

    Information 26

    Support from staff and management 27

    Participation from others 28

  BENCHMARKING TRAPS 29

    There isn't anything else to learn 29

    Justifying the Status Quo 29

    It's all about numbers 30

    Using your Shotgun 30

    Using Published Benchmarking As-Is 31

    Comparing Apples to Apples 31

    No Follow-up 32

    One-Time Effort 32

    Not Setting Your Goals 33

    Your Benchmarking Plan – Goals 34

  COMPARING EFFECTIVELY 36

  OPERATIONAL PRACTICES BENCHMARKING 37

  BEST PRACTICE VERSUS LEADING PRACTICE 40

DEPTH OF BENCHMARKING 41
    Shallow Dive 41
    Deep Dive 42
TYPES OF BENCHMARKING 42
    Broad-Based 42
    Internal 43
    Peer-to-Peer 45
    Your Benchmarking Plan – Benchmarking Types 48
WHAT TO BENCHMARK 50
    Establishing Core Business Requirements 50
    Your Benchmarking Plan – Core Business Requirements 51
WHAT AREAS SHOULD I LOOK AT? 53
    Financial Information 53
    Volume Information/Processes 54
    Operational Practices 56
    Your Benchmarking Plan – Benchmarking Items 59
PRIORITIZING YOUR BENCHMARKING 61
    Your Benchmarking Plan – Prioritizing 62
COLLECTING DATA 64
    Collection Techniques 65
    Broad-Based Benchmarking 66
    Internal benchmarking 66
    Peer-to-Peer Benchmarking 67
COLLECTION TOOLS 68
    Spreadsheets 68
    Forms 70
    Interviews 70
    Analyzing Benchmarking Results 71
    Tools 72
    Pivot Tables and Pivot Charts 74
    Validating 76
MAKING ADJUSTMENTS 78
    Your Benchmarking Plan – Making Adjustments 81
UNDERSTANDING THE NUMBERS 83
    Average/Mean 83

Weighted Average *84*

Median *86*

Percentile *87*

ASSESSING YOUR PERFORMANCE 88

What does Better mean? *88*

Are the gaps real? *89*

Why does the gap exist? *90*

Deciding on the action to take *92*

Your Benchmarking Plan – Your Gaps *94*

SECTION 2 –CONDUCTING BENCHMARKING 95

GENERAL BENCHMARKING PROCESS 96

BROAD-BASED BENCHMARKING 103

Benchmarking Studies *103*

Review available Benchmarks *103*

Gather your Information *103*

Act on the Results *104*

The Next Step *105*

PEER-TO-PEER BENCHMARKING 107

Getting Peer involvement *107*

Decide what to benchmark *110*

Collect and Compare *110*

Analyze the Results *112*

Identify Practices to Adopt *113*

Implement changes *114*

INTERNAL BENCHMARKING 115

SECTION 3 – IMPLEMENTING CHANGE 119

PREPARING FOR CHANGE 120

Start at the Beginning *120*

Prioritize *121*

Selection Process *123*

Selling your Initiative *123*

Your Benchmarking Plan – Dealing With Objections *128*

STRATEGY 129

THE BUSINESS CASE 129

IMPLEMENTATION 131

What are the roadblocks? 131

How can you overcome the roadblocks? 131

What resources do you need? 132

What are the Timelines? 132

What are the main steps to implement your plan? 133

Your Benchmarking Plan – Implementation 134

Introduction

Managers should use benchmarking to assess their department or company performance and to make improvements.

However, the traditional approach for benchmarking is to compare yourself to others using metrics. That approach tells you how you compare, but not how to improve.

You need another way to use benchmarking so that it is useful to you.

A more strategic approach to your benchmarking will provide you with actual practices that you can use or adapt to improve your results.

This book shifts you from benchmarking numbers to benchmarking practices.

Michel Theriault

Michel Theriault

Benchmarking is a Strategic Tool

Benchmarking isn't just an exercise, and it doesn't have to be a large, complex process. Benchmarking is simply about looking at a process, cost, or activity and finding out whether there are better ways to do it. Your benchmarking activity can be as simple as looking at one task at a time to see if there is a more effective way to approach that task.

In fact, it is easier to start small and build towards larger benchmarking exercises. By starting small and providing beneficial changes, you can demonstrate the value of the process and then go on to tackle larger, more difficult benchmarking.

In addition to being a process or exercise, benchmarking is a form of measurement in which you measure against something to see where you might be lacking, to identify the areas, and to take corrective action. This essential approach is supported by results measurement, which is the best way to show your improvements. Measurement is the core of almost all quality management systems."

While benchmarking typically looks backward by measuring and comparing past information, the results of benchmarking should, in fact, be a forward-looking strategic tool that managers can employ to advance their service, their department, and their career.

One challenge to getting approval and funding for new initiatives that improve ongoing results is having facts and data to support a new business case. Your benchmarking exercise can supply evidence that supports a new model, identifying results that others have achieved and documenting how you can achieve similar results.

Benefits of Benchmarking

Benchmarking isn't just an academic exercise, and it isn't just about knowing where you stand compared to others.

Effective benchmarking is about using information to make improvements.

Some of the key benefits of benchmarking include:

➡ Comparison of non-financial performance to learn how results are achieved so you can adopt the more effective practices.

➡ Comparison of financial results to identify what organizations are performing with lower costs, to explore the reasons of those lower costs, and to adopt the corresponding processes that work for your organization.

➡ Comparison of results for services to identify how to augment your existing performance management processes and to enable comparison between your services and those of another company.

➡ Comparison of your staffing levels with others to either gauge the efficiency and effectiveness of your team or to build a case for additional resources.

➡ Comparison of your tools and processes with others so you can justify your initiatives for process change or improvement or to acquire the tools, such as computerized systems, that you require.

Using This Book

This benchmarking book is designed to provide the processes, tools, and information that you need to implement your own benchmarking exercise.

While this book covers the fundamentals of benchmarking and provides details that you can apply, your specific situation or requirements might require some adjustments to the approach or the processes. This book gives you the information and the background you need so you understand specific situations and can make those adjustments with confidence.

Real-world examples are provided in key areas throughout the book, so you can see how to apply the principles and approaches.

In addition, this book includes questions at the end of each major topic, which will help you develop your own approach based on the principles in the book. You can print or copy the question page and fill it in or simply answer the questions in a separate document, which can become the starting point for your benchmarking exercise.

What you should learn:

- ✓ When to benchmark
- ✓ How benchmarking can help
- ✓ Which benchmarking approach to use
- ✓ What information to collect
- ✓ How to analyze benchmarking information
- ✓ How to establish an action plan that is related to the benchmarking results

✓ How to communicate results to get funding or approvals that are needed for change

The book is divided into 3 sections.

Within each section is a series of questions for you to answer. These won't test your memory about what you have read; they are designed to help you think about how to apply the principles you've read about.

Section 1 - Foundations of Benchmarking

This section provides the key information that you need to understand benchmarking. It covers traditional benchmarking, expands on strategic benchmarking approaches, results based benchmarking and on the three main types of benchmarking: broad-based, internal and peer-to-peer benchmarking.

This section also discusses benchmarking at different detail levels, what to benchmark, types of required information, data collection, and how to analyze benchmarking results.

Section 2 - Conducting Benchmarking

This section builds on information from the Foundations of Benchmarking section and gives you detailed steps, processes, and other practical information that you can use with each of the three main benchmarking processes: broad-based, internal, and peer-to-peer.

Section 3 - Implementing Change

This section helps you make changes because the reason you conduct benchmarking is to identify areas you should change to improve results. This section discusses how to prepare for those changes, how to develop an action plan to implement the changes you want, and how to sell your changes and the benchmarking results to senior management so you can get your implementation plan approved.

Section 1 – Foundations of Benchmarking

This section covers the foundations of benchmarking, including the information, techniques, and approaches that you need to implement your own benchmarking initiative.

The next section will look at specific processes for three main types of benchmarking initiatives.

Benchmarking For Results

The word "benchmark" simply means something you compare against. In the strictest sense, you would make that comparison and identify whether your results were higher or lower (i.e. better or worst) than the benchmark.

For benchmarking to be effective, however, you also need to understand the reasons you were higher or lower than the benchmark and whether the benchmark you identified is a benchmark you wish to achieve.

If, indeed, you want to achieve the benchmark's results, you would implement the changes necessary to improve your results.

This procedure is why benchmarking is not just a numbers exercise. Benchmarking is all about process, tools, and resources that achieve results and establishing the results that you should implement to achieve the results your organization requires.

Effective benchmarking should help you identify the things that you should and should not be doing to get best results. Part of that process is identifying your own corporate goals and ensuring that when you compare your results with others, you take those goals into account.

For instance, just because another organization has a lower cost for maintenance services doesn't necessarily mean that is the benchmark you want to achieve. That lower cost might be a result of practices or service levels that are lower than your organization wants to implement. Therefore, you can't simply compare the numbers and state that you should lower your costs. You need to understand the practices and your goals and adjust accordingly.

Example

An organization's cost is at the lowest end of the range compared to the benchmarking results from comparable organizations. If you look only at financial results, it could appear that this organization is highly efficient. Instead, the fact that it appears among the companies with the lowest cost might indicate a possible problem currently or in the future because they are not spending enough money. You need to also analyze results and other issues. For instance, low costs in retail store maintenance could cause low customer experience ratings.

And benchmarking is not always just the direct comparison between your organization and others. You also need to gather information that lets you adjust the benchmarking results to make them more comparable.

For instance, if you are comparing the cost of a predominantly labor-intensive service, such as guards, cleaning, or even landscaping, you might want to know the base labor costs either for the organizations or the regions where you're doing the comparison. This additional information would help you to analyze your total cost for the service and to be sure that when you determine what improvements or changes to make, the costs involved are things you have direct control over.

Energy presents a similar cost issue. Comparing costs of energy between jurisdictions can be difficult due to different pricing. In addition, weather impacts the amount of energy consumed as well as the costs, so you need to have comparative information to effectively adjust consumption and cost information so that you can take out things you have no control over, such as the weather.

Why Benchmark?

You benchmark to identify areas where you could improve results by adopting other organizations' practices to achieve better results than you are currently achieving.

In any organization, there are areas where you may be excelling, but there are also areas where you could improve. No organization excels at everything or in every function that it performs and can benefit from learning where its performance sits relative to others, and what kind of practices and changes it can make to improve its performance.

Don't just benchmark because you discover a problem with your costs or other performance-related metrics. You should benchmark on a regular basis simply because it is the right strategic business approach for managers to adopt.

Of course, the real practical purpose to benchmarking is an evidence-based approach that lets you establish facts and data that support your business case for change and improvement in your department.

This evidence doesn't always mean reductions in costs or resources to meet the lower metrics of other organizations.

In fact, benchmarking can point to areas where you are not performing as well as you might because you do not have the necessary resources or funding. An effective benchmarking approach digs deeper than just cost information, so you can identify those areas, build a strong business case, and enhance your service delivery, mitigate risk, and deliver results.

Even if you think you are doing everything right, how do you know unless you compare? No organization is the best at everything, and the same is true for yours.

So, if you aren't benchmarking, you can't possibly be doing everything you should be doing.

Identify superior performance to emulate

A benchmarking exercise can help you identify the processes and practices that others use to achieve superior performance. The first step is to identify who has superior performance and then subsequently identify the reasons why that performance is superior.

Learn about leading practices

Without a benchmarking process, you can't be sure whether or not somebody else's practices are likely to achieve superior performance. By first benchmarking numbers and then determining the practices behind those numbers, you and your organization can learn from others and add subsequent value to your efforts.

The important thing to note here is the term 'leading practices' instead of 'best practices' because the practices used by others might not be, in fact, the best practices for you to adopt. Part of your exercise is to determine whether those practices would meet the goals and objectives within your own organization before you either adopt those practices or decide that the benchmark results achieved by others should be your goal.

Ask tough questions and show where you should focus

The simple process of benchmarking helps you ask tough questions that you might not otherwise ask about your own practices and processes. As indicated earlier, no manager can claim to do everything in the most effective way. Benchmarking is one means through which you can identify things that others are doing that you aren't and pinpoint areas you should focus on. Without this comparison, your ability to implement the most effective practices within your organization is limited.

Document evidence for business justification

While many managers are fearful of what the benchmarking results might show about their own performance, the reality is that this information is one of your best tools for justifying new initiatives and business cases that will improve results.

Typically, business results are based on existing tools, resources, and processes that were put in place some time ago. After documenting your benchmarking results, you have evidence to convince senior management to invest in new tools, resources, or processes to achieve higher-level results. You will also have grounds upon which to convince your team to change processes and practices that it has been using for years.

With an effective benchmarking process, you will have evidence and numbers that you can use to convince senior management and get your staff on-board. Without this evidence, they are seldom interested in investing or supporting new initiatives.

What is Benchmarking Not?

Benchmarking isn't just about numbers. You don't just compare numbers and, if your results are average or better, keep on doing what you've always done. For one, do you really want your organization to be average?

Example

A manager conducted benchmarking that showed his results were average compared with the benchmarking results. This information was used to justify the status quo, and no further action was taken.

Benchmarking should be a learning process, not just a measurement exercise. You should effectively compare the benchmarking results and then dig deep to understand what you can do differently. Even if our organization's results are average, that means that others are doing something different and getting better results. You need to find out what they are doing.

Think about several runners who run a race and finish with the same time. All runners have excellent technique except for runner number 2. If you benchmark their times, you would say the second runner did well and that would be the end of it. In fact, you shouldn't be satisfied only with how the numbers make the runners look. Focus on more than just their times. Compare their techniques and related performance in various stages of the race, such as the start. You might discover that, at one stage, one runner's technique is poor and, with improvement in technique, that runner could easily win next time.

Remember, benchmarking isn't just about numbers; it's about learning and improving.

Traditional versus Strategic Benchmarking

To get the best results from your benchmarking exercise, you need to recognize the difference between traditional benchmarking and strategic benchmarking. It's essentially the difference between a numbers exercise and a results-based exercise.

You need to be aware of both benchmarking types and might, in fact, use both depending on the situation. Traditional benchmarking is usually the place to start, after which you implement strategic benchmarking.

Traditional Benchmarking

Traditionally, benchmarking has been characterized almost exclusively by a focus on numbers. Most broad-based benchmarking exercises are conducted with numbers as their central point, which is why you sometimes need to dig a little deeper into the details or conduct your own internal or peer-to-peer benchmarking.

Traditional benchmarking enables you to compare results of some kind, whether in dollars or numbers, so you know where you stand compared to others. This measurement could include cost for staff, materials, finished unit costs, rework, delivery time, response time, process time, sales, staffing numbers by volume and more.

Traditional benchmarking has a great deal of value because it can be done fairly easily and can identify areas where you should focus your attention.

However, this type of benchmarking typically only enables you to know which direction you need to travel so you can achieve results, like using a compass. It does not give you enough information about what you need to do to achieve those results.

Strategic Benchmarking

Strategic benchmarking takes your analysis to the next level. Usually building on broad-based benchmarking results, this type of benchmarking digs deeper into the practices and processes that others use to get superior results.

Strategic benchmarking is a much more complex and time-consuming process, so, instead of addressing a broad range of benchmarks, you usually focus on a specific area, service, or process. Then you dig deeper into the results, processes, resources, and other issues that help you identify things you can do to improve your own results.

This type of benchmarking doesn't just tell you the direction you need to take; it should provide you with the route to take, like a roadmap. This usually includes new processes, tools, techniques, resources, and other initiatives that you have learned from the organizations included in the benchmarking exercise.

Your Benchmarking Plan – Your Experience

Questions:

1. What benchmarking have you already conducted?

2. What did it tell you?

3. What issues did you encounter?

4. What more can you do?

5. If you did benchmarking again, what would you do differently?

Notes

_____

_____

_____

_____

_____

_____

_____

_____

_____

_____

_____

Prerequisites for Benchmarking

Simply conducting a benchmarking exercise isn't enough. You and your organization need to be prepared for the benchmarking exercise and anticipated outcome. You should have not only a purpose for your benchmarking, but an approach that enables you to implement the changes that you identify from your benchmarking exercise.

Information

To do effective benchmarking of any kind, you need to have the information on what to benchmark. If you have participated in an industry benchmarking exercise, you know the kind of information that is required for this broad-based benchmarking. If you haven't participated in industry benchmarking, you should consider participating or, at the very least, get the benchmarking survey form or the benchmarking report so you know the kind of information that is involved.

When you go beyond the traditional broad-based benchmarking and focus on a specific area for more strategic benchmarking, you require the right kind of information with the right level of detail.

For instance, when analyzing costs, you need financial information that goes beyond a handful of major line items.

As an example, your maintenance and repair accounts should be sub-divided into categories such as internal labor, external contracts, standing contracts, supplies and materials, professional and consulting fees, permits. You should even differentiate between minor maintenance and major maintenance activities.

The level of detail that you can achieve directly impacts your ability to analyze benchmarking results. Of course, when you benchmark against other organizations, it is important to have the same level of information about them as with your company This should be a prerequisite for selecting partners for peer-to-peer benchmarking.

Beyond simply having the information, you need to be able to understand it, so you can make adjustments that provide equal comparison. This issue will be described further later in this book.

Support from staff and management

In some cases, you will be able to conduct benchmarking without support from your staff and senior management; however, in most cases, you will need their support.

Since effective benchmarking isn't just about numbers, your staff will provide some valuable information and background that will help you analyze and compare the data, so you can determine which practices you should change or adopt. Your staff might also be better equipped than you are to determine which information is comparable and what adjustments need to be made in order to effectively compare different organizations. Getting staff involved in the process also makes it easier to get their buy-in and support for changes.

Having support from senior management before you begin the benchmarking process makes it more likely that you will convince them to implement the resulting required changes. As mentioned before, you should not fear results that show your operation to be less efficient. Instead, you should take this opportunity to drive change that will improve your efficiency. By preparing your senior management to expect new initiatives and business cases arising from your your benchmarking exercise, you are more likely to be successful with your changes.

Participation from others

As soon as you go beyond broad-based benchmarking exercises, you need the active participation from colleagues in other organizations. Getting their participation is the only way you can do the detailed benchmarking that identifies specific practices and procedures to adopt.

Other managers need to have the same objectives and dedication to the benchmarking exercise as you do. They also need to be able to share information and to have the required level of detail to effectively benchmark. Keep in mind that the benchmarking exercise does not need to be a highly formal activity, and it can be much more informal if you're trying to focus on a particular issue or topic. Additionally, you might not need to share detailed financial information depending on what you're trying to benchmark.

Some tips and approaches to getting active participation from your peers in the industry are discussed later in this book.

Benchmarking Traps

As discussed, benchmarking is a valuable tool for managers to make improvements to their operations. Moving from the more traditional approach to benchmarking toward a strategic approach provides increased benefits to the exercise.

Unfortunately, there are many traps that are easy to fall into. The following are key traps you should avoid and that you should be on the lookout for when you're implementing a benchmarking exercise with your peers.

There isn't anything else to learn

If you think you know all there is to know already and are using the best practices and approaches, you won't do what it takes to Benchmark effectively. Admitting that you can't possibly know it all and that others may be doing some things better is critical to moving benchmarking from a numbers exercise to a process that adds value to your organization.

Justifying the Status Quo

Some people use benchmarking results simply to justify the status quo. Since raw benchmarking results can be deceptive, justifying the status quo is easy to accomplish. You need to understand how the results have been compiled, the sample size, the type of organization, location, services, and more to effectively compare data.

You must benchmark with the intent to improve, not to justify the status quo. Don't be complacent if you happen to fall within published average benchmarks.

Do you really want to be average, or do you want to be a leader? Learn from what the others are doing and implement change in any areas where you don't lead.

It's all about numbers

Benchmarking isn't just comparing numbers. It's a process of identifying where you can improve and learning new approaches, processes, and techniques that leading organizations use and that you can apply to improve your results. Comparing your results with a benchmark number is only the starting point for benchmarking.

The next step includes benchmarking practices and even processes to understand how results are being accomplished so you can determine whether they are applicable to your own situation and adopt or adapt them.

Using your Shotgun

You have limited time and energy, so focus your benchmarking on key areas that will have a large impact. You can always return to other areas later. You can start with a quick exercise that covers most areas and use its results to focus your more in-depth issues, to identify areas of importance to your organization, or to single out areas you feel are already lagging and focus on those. After you have gone through the first benchmarking exercise, which moves from comparing numbers to assessing procedures, systems, and resources, and then to implementing change, you can move to other areas and apply what you previously learned to them, which will lead to continual improvement.

Using Published Benchmarking As-Is

Generic published benchmarking results provide good information from which to identify areas for further study, but, even at a high-level, you need to be careful with the comparisons. Carefully review the methodology that was used and look at the sample size and participant profiles. You might need to adjust the information based on your specific situation, geography, and more. For costing, be sure the generic results include the same information you do in the comparisons and adjust as necessary. For staffing levels, assess the functions and titles, and be sure of the roles and responsibilities. Look closely at the sample sizes, number of participants, and volumes if applicable. These categories can be misleading and provide unsuitable comparisons.

If you do your own surveys, be clear about what information you are looking for. Ask the right questions and build in the ability to identify unique issues that will affect your comparisons. Expand your survey beyond simple costing numbers and include process, systems, and resourcing when possible. Alternately, this type of information can be gathered in a follow-up survey or direct discussion with organizations that appear to be the best match.

Comparing Apples to Apples

Everybody talks about not comparing apples to oranges, but the bigger risk is the more subtle differences between apples. Accurate comparison is not as easy as it seems, and using averages provided in published benchmarks can be misleading and lead to incorrect decisions.

You don't want to compare apples to oranges for sure, but you also don't want to compare a Golden Delicious apple with a Macintosh one. To get a proper comparison, you need to assess each component and compare things that are the same. You might even need to make adjustments to ensure an equal comparison. The similarity of comparisons is important because many factors are at play.

No Follow-up

You need to start your benchmarking with a clear willingness and ability to make necessary changes that are based on the benchmarking information and analysis. If you are not, your benchmarking exercise will be wasted. Follow-up includes getting the support you need from senior management and making the effort to develop action and implementation plans to make even small changes. Incremental change is just as important as transformational change.

One-Time Effort

Benchmarking isn't just a one-time exercise to complete and forget. After you benchmark, you should continue internal measurements. Compare your new results with the benchmark results and with your own historical results to see how you are trending and to identify any appropriate action if you start to slip. Periodically, drill down again to look at procedures, processes, and resources for key benchmarks to see whether you can make more changes to improve results. As necessary, focus on a new area.

Not Setting Your Goals

The first step before you start benchmarking is to be clear on why you are doing it and how you will use the results. These objectives will dictate how to structure and manage your benchmarking exercise for the best results.

Goal setting also includes what categories to prioritize. When you move beyond traditional benchmarking, you need to focus on the areas where you are most likely to get the best results, not only where you can get the benchmarking information. Use broad-based benchmarking information first to identify areas where you are lagging or merely average. Then, consider your own organization's priorities to establish your goals.

For instance, the broad-based benchmarking information might reveal areas where you could decrease costs, but reliability, customer experience, or other factors might be the most critical priorities for your organization. Start with them.

When you decide on your goals, consider what the outcomes might be, the decisions that you might want to make before you start, and the steps you will take to investigate in more depth to determine what changes to implement. Align these actions with your senior management so you are more likely to be able to implement change.

If you don't think you can make changes or influence your results, rethink the priorities or find ways to make those changes happen. Use the results to push change and make your case within the organization.

Your Benchmarking Plan – Goals

Use this table to determine your initial goals and objectives for your exercise. Remember, you may reassess or reprioritize them as you go along.

Priority	Goal	Issues	Anticipated Outcomes

Notes

Comparing Effectively

Accurately comparing results and measurements is not as easy as it seems and using statistical information can sometimes result in wrong decisions.

Given that you have decided to benchmark and clearly understand why, you can focus your attention on the areas that are most important. And you can make meaningful comparisons that lead you to more detailed information, which you can make decisions on.

For any detailed benchmarking exercise, you need to assess each component or measurement and compare the situations, then make adjustments to ensure an equal comparison. The similarity is important because many factors influence costs and results.

You might need to adjust any of the following factors:

- ✓ Hours of operation
- ✓ Geographic location/distribution
- ✓ Portfolio/size
- ✓ Type of use
- ✓ Local legislation and costs
- ✓ Local resources and practices
- ✓ Core business objectives

These issues and how to deal with them are discussed in more detail further below.

Operational Practices Benchmarking

As mentioned, traditional benchmarking typically compares numbers from only a broad base of benchmarking participants. This approach is a good starting point if you are comparing the right things, but for strategic benchmarking, you must expand the vision to operational issues, including processes, procedures, and more. Looking at these operational items can explain why you are performing well in some places and can offer reasons to maintain the status quo in those places. These operational items can also explain why you are not performing well in other places and can offer reasons to change those actions. This operational approach is often taken in conjunction with more traditional financial benchmarking.

You need to look at operational issues beyond simple costs and volume metrics because these operational items often drive cost and volume metrics in your department. An inefficient process can introduce bottlenecks into the system and can negatively affect costs, speed of service delivery, and customer service. If any of these three items are critical to your organization's success, benchmarking your process, people, or systems could find areas for improvement.

Operational benchmarking can include the following:

➡ Systems that are being used (logistics, maintenance, sales, inventory, etc.)
➡ Staffing levels
➡ Qualifications/training
➡ Balance between in-house and contracted resources
➡ Quality assurance processes
➡ Customer satisfaction processes
➡ Maintenance management processes
➡ Organization and staffing models
➡ Procedures and tasks

Compare your processes, people, and systems with other high-performing organizations so you can understand what they do differently. Then, assess whether you can emulate their success and implement it. The biggest mistake you can make is assuming you are doing everything you should be doing and doing it well. In fact, there is always someone else who is doing something better, and you can learn from them – even if your benchmarking results look good.

Operational benchmarking should identify the areas where you are already achieving the right level, the areas where you are not achieving the right level, and the changes you can implement to make improvements. That's why simply knowing the cost information, for instance, is not enough. Instead of simply knowing that you are high or low relative to others, you need to understand what they are doing differently to achieve their results, so you can implement those changes. In some cases, you might find that the higher performers either have advantages that you can't emulate (i.e. local labour costs) or core business goals that you don't want to emulate (i.e. image, risk of failure, etc.)

Evaluating your operations is critical to your success. Operational benchmarking tells you whether your operations are as efficient and effective as possible and identifies things you can do to enable you to serve your corporation's core needs better.

When your department is part of a larger organization, but isn't the core business, it is challenging to identify where you can be as effective and efficient as possible, and you might be at a disadvantage because you won't have as much built-in comparisons available to you, depending on your portfolio size.

As the department of an organization, you have less opportunity for exposure to other methods, procedures, and latest practices because you might not have many peers in your organization to interact with and learn from. Also, your supervisors and other senior members of your organization might not have knowledge and experience in your profession that they can share with you or provide guidance for. You might be the sole champion and sole knowledge source for your role in your organization

Despite the challenges that you can face as a sole champion and knowledge source, taking benchmarking to the operational level can provide important information about the organization's efficiency and effectiveness. This information, in turn, can help you deliver the services and results that your organization needs for its core business success.

Best Practice versus Leading Practice

As indicated, benchmarking can help you identify practices that others are doing that you can emulate to improve results.

While some call these "best practices", they might in fact not be the best practices for you. A better way to look at practices that others use to achieve superior performance is "leading practices" Simply put, the best practice for one organization might not be the best practice for yours.

It's possible that other organizations are using practices that would be detrimental to your organization and your goals. For instance, low maintenance costs might be the result of a minimalist approach to maintenance that an organization takes with a short-term view rather than a long-term view. Or these low costs might result in a business where a system failure carries little risk, and the business model makes it preferable to pay for a repair when it is needed instead of spending money for prevention.

Before you consider adopting a practice, carefully assess the impact to your organization's goals and objectives. The practice might result in a low cost or high efficiency that you would like to emulate, but it could have a detrimental effect.

Depth of Benchmarking

One of the differences between traditional and strategic benchmarking is how deep you go in your benchmarking initiative.

The graphic shows the range of benchmarking related to the level of detail by different types of benchmarking initiatives.

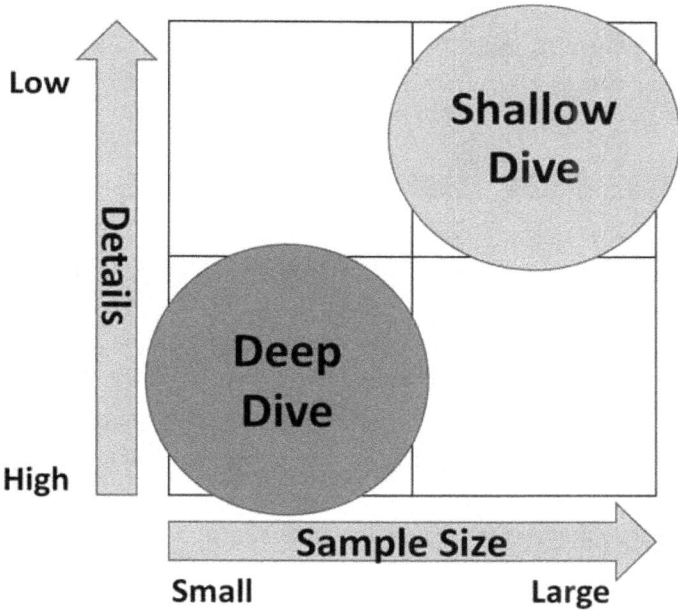

Shallow Dive

Most broad-based benchmarking is relatively shallow because it looks at a broad set of metrics compiled at a relatively high level. In some cases, there might be additional detail available; however, typically you won't have the level of detail needed to do a detailed exercise, particularly to identify the practices used by top performers.

Deep Dive

A deep dive involves going into more detail in the benchmarking exercise and looking at the practices behind the results. A deeper dive requires more data and information, usually with a smaller sample size. Because it does require more effort, you usually focus on one area of interest rather than a broad range of areas.

Types of Benchmarking

As discussed previously, there are three types of benchmarking: broad-based, internal, and peer-to-peer. The depth and level of details for each of these types can vary. Where possible, you should apply each of these types in succession, starting with broad-based benchmarking, then internal benchmarking if your portfolio lends itself to this type, then peer-to-peer based benchmarking, focusing on the areas that the first two types identified.

You can do the first two types quickly and efficiently as long as the final peer-to-peer based benchmarking is done with more detail and effort.

Broad-Based

The best example of this benchmarking type is typified by industry benchmarking reports. You can quickly assess your results against a cross section of other organizations that participated in the benchmarking exercise across a wide range of metrics.

The information is segmented and sorted based on a number of different criteria that the participating organizations provided, which enables you to compare your organization with those included in the report with more certainty.

For instance, you can look at the results over the entire benchmarking sample, then look at only the results that are for similar businesses or situations or regions as yours. For costing, you can do the same, and usually you can even make comparisons within your geographic area, based on the regions collected in the benchmarking exercise. This aspect is particularly important because costing can vary between regions and countries for external reasons, regardless of your efficiency and practices.

Even with broad-based benchmarking it is important that you are comparing the same information, for instance, you should ensure that the correct measurement method is used for the outputs and that the right costs in various categories are included or excluded.

Internal

Internal benchmarking makes comparisons within your own organization. These comparisons can be between different teams, regions, service providers, processes, practices, and initiatives.

Instead of comparing your consolidated results as you would with a broad-based benchmark, with internal benchmarking, you compare unconsolidated results within your own portfolio. Of course, for smaller organizations, this comparison is generally impractical; however, you might find areas where you can apply this technique.

The biggest benefit of internal benchmarking is that you should have ready access to the data. As mentioned earlier, if your data is not detailed enough, your benchmarking initiative will have limited results when it comes to analyzing specifics. If you find you are not tracking the kind of information you need to do effective benchmarking, your first objective is to implement measurement and tracking processes.

To begin internal benchmarking, do a numbers comparison; then, based on the results of that comparison, investigate further to determine what might be different within your portfolio that presents you with different results. The cause might be the approach taken by personnel, interpretation of process, local adjustments to process, local tools and techniques used to manage, emphasis or skills of different staff members, or a number of other factors. Frequently, even when an organization is supposed to have common practices, procedures, training, and more, individuals who manage different parts of the business might have found different ways to accomplish the same activities that are either more or less effective.

While your quality assurance process should help you identify where your processes are not followed and highlight areas that can be emulated, achieving these ends through a benchmarking approach is better than relying on the quality assurance process that you have in place, which generally is designed to serve a different purpose.

For instance, if you are measuring the time to respond to and close out work orders and find that in some locations you have a much shorter timeframe than others, you can investigate the practices used at those locations to see whether or not these practices should be applied everywhere. Naturally, in some cases the practices are localized and might not be applicable elsewhere. This circumstance is a similar to the concept that we noted previously, "best practices" use by others might not apply to your organization. The point here is to find out what practices are being followed and to determine whether those practices can be implemented elsewhere to improve results.

Peer-to-Peer

Peer-to-peer benchmarking can be one of the more challenging techniques, yet it will produce the best results from your benchmarking exercise. It is usually done on a more detailed level than broad-based benchmarking, requires the full cooperation of your colleagues, and requires you to do the detailed comparative analysis, validation of data, and adjustments that would've been done by others in broad-based benchmarking.

However, you can choose to benchmark a very specific element of operations, thereby narrowing and reducing the required level of activity. After you've gone through the process once, it will be much easier to do it again for a different area with the same peers.

There are usually two challenges involved in peer-to-peer benchmarking. First, you must convince your peers to cooperate with you, so they will share their results with you. Second, you must organize the data into a structure and format, so you can make an effective comparison. Of course, this data doesn't include just basic metrics information; it also includes the practices and procedures that your peers use to achieve the results.

Example

In a peer-to-peer benchmarking exercise, various practices were reviewed to see if any correlated with the results for maintenance costs. The clearest correlation was the number of separate job classifications for maintenance positions at each organization. The higher the number, the higher the costs. It appeared that the higher number of classifications meant less flexibility with staffing and resource allocation, resulting in higher costs.

This means benchmarking is not just a collection exercise for data, it requires structured discussions and interviews that allow you to compare the approaches, practices, tools, systems, staffing, etc. with your peers. You might start the exercise, get all the information you think you require and analyze and review the practices - only to realize that you need more information. Be sure to set the expectations with your peers before you begin the process.

When choosing the organizations that you want to benchmark with, don't select only organizations that are clear leaders or are virtually identical to your own organization. A diverse group of benchmarking partners can provide a rich store of information that you could miss if you limit your selections to organizations similar to your own. By including several diverse organizations in your benchmarking exercise, you are likely to find practices you can implement. Remember, it's not just about comparing the metrics; it's about learning and applying practices.

In fact, the peer-to-peer benchmarking process should be a non-judgmental comparison, focused less on specific metrics and more on organization structure, systems, access to expertise, service delivery models, practices and procedures, systems, information, and functionality.

Your Benchmarking Plan – Benchmarking Types

Questions

Do you have information you can compare with available broad-based benchmarking? If so, what is it?

What Do You Have?	What Benchmarking Results Are Available?

Is your organization large enough to do internal benchmarking? If so, what areas could you compare?

What to Compare	Between What?

Do you know other managers or other organizations that you would like to do a peer-to-peer benchmarking exercise with?

Organization	Reasons

Notes

_____

_____

_____

_____

_____

_____

_____

_____

_____

_____

What to Benchmark

Before you start your benchmarking process, you need to decide what you're going to benchmark. Usually, these are activities, processes and results that matter to your organization, that you have control over, and that you believe you can change.

Establishing Core Business Requirements

Since your benchmarking exercise is ultimately to improve services and results that either serve or have a significant impact on your organization's core business, the first step is to determine how your department impacts that core business.

Identify the core business requirements of your organization and then list one or more services or activities that your department provides that impacts the core business. Then you can identify what you should benchmark to improve results.

You need to establish a clear understanding of your impact and importance to the organization's core business to help you evaluate and then prioritize your initiatives.

Then, when you benchmark, you are in a better position to assess the results in your own context and priorities.

Your Benchmarking Plan – Core Business Requirements

Questions

What core business activities do you potentially impact and what can you benchmark to assess whether you are achieving the required results. The core business activities will help identify the items that you need to benchmark and any additional information.

➡ **Core business requirements** – What are the business requirements that ensure success?
➡ **Department impact** – What is your part in supporting the core business requirements?
➡ **Primary measurement** – What are the main measures of success that can identify what to benchmark?
➡ **Supporting information** – What items support the primary measurement, such as practices, resources, or systems that might drive the benchmark results?

Notes

_____

_____

_____

_____

_____

_____

_____

_____

_____

_____

_____

_____

_____

_____

_____

_____

_____

_____

_____

What areas should I look at?

Now that you've identified the core business requirements for your organization, the impact your department has on them, and how you can measure success, you can focus on the specific areas of service delivery within your organization that you should look at to improve results.

Naturally, you should always benchmark costs along with other performance-related information, because costs are a significant issue with most organizations and they are often linked to results.

Financial Information

Benchmarking financial information is one of the most common benchmarking activities. However, beyond simply revealing whether you're more or less expensive than others, it doesn't usually give you any clear indication of what you should change, since costs are ultimately driven from operational practices.

So, although comparing financial information is important, you need to benchmark other information as described below, so you can understand what you might need to do to reduce costs to the point where they balance with your priorities and requirements. It's also important to understand your organization relative to others and to appreciate the drivers of the financial information, so you can compare effectively.

For instance, comparing the cost of landscaping and snow removal services at your buildings means you need information about the area being landscaped or cleared of snow as well as the weather factors, such as the number of snowfalls, total snowfall, growing season, etc. This complexity explains why comparing financial information.

In this case, even the use of the building (warehouse, school, office) can impact the comparison. This is you might be better off looking at the practices, such as procurement practices, equipment, tools, staffing methods, standards, etc.

When benchmarking costs, it's important to measure costs relative to an appropriate base. When you compare with peers, ensure that you are using the same standard as they did.

Usually you can compare financial costs to volume, such as the cost per customer, cost per unit, cost per hour, cost per phone call and more. If you manage unique services or responsibilities with their own type of volume information, perhaps based on your company's core business, you can make comparisons relative to their base. Be aware, however, that it might be more difficult to find comparable information on which to benchmark, particularly because many organizations simply don't accurately track the type of information you need.

Volume Information/Processes

After you move past financial benchmarking, or even in support of your financial benchmarking, the next step is to look at volume and process-related metrics.

Since many of these metrics will have an impact on costing, it's prudent to look at them together when possible, which might lead you to look at other factors, such as practices.

For instance, if you were responsible for moves and relocations within your organization, you can assess those costs relative to your total square feet of office space or number of staff. A high number of moves is one driver of the costs, but your practices related to office furniture, configuration, and allocation might be what you really need to look at in order to identify changes that you can implement.

Directly comparable information between your organization and others can e challenging, since many factors can influence volume, process metrics, and whether you're more or less efficient than other organizations. For instance, the density of your office (square feet or square meters per person) can have an impact on various things like cleaning supply costs, security, work order call volume, and more.

The ability to adjust for these differences is one way you can compare more effectively. We discuss this in Section 2 - Conducting Benchmarking.

Example

In a benchmarking exercise, the staffing levels in a team appear to be in-line with the broad-based benchmark. However, the same benchmark information showed significant differences in work volume. This difference in volume actually indicates an under-staffing of resources and a higher efficiency than the benchmark.

Operational Practices

Practices relate to how you do things. They go beyond the financial costs or the volume comparisons and enable you to compare your tools, policies, resources, and even the processes you use to achieve results. This information is important to determine what you need to do, change, or stop doing, to match the results others are achieving.

It's not as useful to benchmark practices on their own as it is to benchmark them in relation to other benchmarking elements. Typically, benchmarking practices supports financial and volume/process benchmarking results. While you might find out about things others are doing that you might want to implement, you won't be able to relate those practices to real performance, which is the objective.

Where possible, link practices to the volume and financial information necessary to determine whether or not those practices are achieving efficient results and allow your results to guide you to the practices that you should adopt or change.

When we talk about practices, it's not just about specific front-line management activities. You need to consider backroom support processes within your department as well as organizational processes and practices that can impact your ability to perform your services efficiently and effectively. These additional elements can include thing such as your HR processes, communications, scheduling, quality assurance, technology interfaces, support from other departments, and other aspects that support your success.

Example

One organization discovered that their dispatch process was causing issues: Technicians were going on-site without sufficient knowledge of the requirements, so they often needed to make a second trip with the correct tools or materials. The process caused a much longer time interval between call and close out and a costlier charge.

Using the cost of office moves as an example, you might find that your cost per move is high and by comparing practices, discover that the low-cost organizations have furniture standards and configurations that reduce or eliminate reconfigurations and changes to partitions and workspaces, which result in lower-cost moves.

When you benchmark operational practices, look at everything, ranging from your policies, processes, forms, training, tasks, roles and and more. For human resources, ask whether you have the right number of staff doing the right tasks and are they trained in the things you need to do?

An example of assessing human resources is project management, which requires a specific set of skills and knowledge as well as a certain kind of person well suited to the role. The wrong fit, combined with poor processes and systems, can have a negative impact on success

Assess what your team spends its time doing. While you don't need to do a detailed time-in-motion study, do a broad-based assessment of the team's functions and the time spent doing tasks, managing contractors, doing administration work, attending meetings, and even traveling. You can use a questionnaire format that asks each team member to estimate time spent on key functions.

Look at job descriptions next and assess whether they still match your needs and whether they match what your staff is doing. Then, look at the resumes and background of the individuals you have doing that work and see whether they match. You can also interview the staff to discover individual interests and observations about the work. This is your opportunity to identify areas where training is required or shifts in responsibilities would suit individual's interests and capabilities better so they can do a better job.

Benchmarking that reveals issues you can act on requires more than just comparing numbers. It involves comparing and assessing operational practices to identify practices you should use to improve results.

Your Benchmarking Plan – Benchmarking Items

Questions

Based on the core business requirements and impacts, what measurements and benchmarking items have you selected to consider benchmarking?

Financial

Volume/Processes

Operational Practices

| |
| |
| |
| |
| |

Notes

Prioritizing Your Benchmarking

After you pick the elements you want to benchmark based on your organization's core business requirements, prioritize these elements, then you can begin to look at the specific measures that you want to compare with others. This process will help you to identify things that you can change and goes beyond simply looking at cost-related items.

While the list of elements you want to benchmark will be different for every organization, there are some common considerations that you can use when determining what to look at.

1.   Start with the higher priority services/activities.

2.   Focus on areas that are known problems or present the greatest risk.

3.   Identify things within your control.

4.   Determine whether you will have the information needed to benchmark those areas.

Your Benchmarking Plan – Prioritizing

Questions

Based on the process of identifying measures and benchmarks to consider, the next step is to prioritize.

Use a table similar to the one shown below and place the benchmark items into the boxes based on whether they deliver high or low value/results and whether it will take a high or low effort to make changes.

The items in the top right quadrant are your most likely targets that you should start with. The bottom left quadrant are those you probably shouldn't bother with, at least initially.

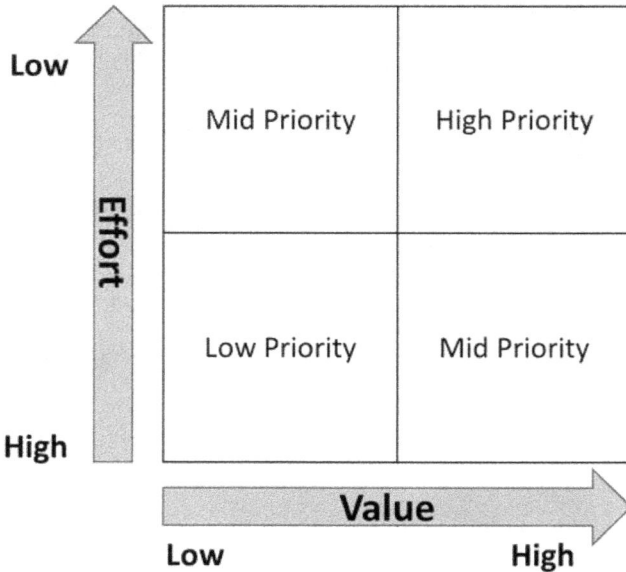

	Mid Priority	High Priority
Effort	Low Priority	Mid Priority

Low ← Effort → High

Value: Low → High

Notes

_____

_____

_____

_____

_____

_____

_____

_____

_____

_____

_____

_____

_____

_____

_____

_____

_____

Collecting Data

At the core of any benchmarking exercise is data collection. While the work leading up to data collection can take a considerable amount of time, data collection has the potential to absorb even more time and energy.

The key reason is the unavailability of data that is formatted and structured the way you need it for effectively comparison between organizations. The second problem is simply not having the data in the first place.

If you are comparing with broad-based benchmarking, the process might be easier because you are compiling only your own information. However, for peer-to-peer benchmarking, data collection might be a challenging task. For internal benchmarking, you should have consistent and useable information, where it exists.

The time and effort necessary for data collection are two of the reasons it's best to focus your benchmarking exercise on the top priorities that you've identified. After you've completed work on the top priorities, you can extend your benchmarking to the next, lower-priority, items.

As discussed, using data to analyze and identify how you compare to other organizations is only a small part of benchmarking's value. The most important part of benchmarking is using the comparison to discover how you can improve your performance. To do this, you need to collect data that supports your initiative.

After you determine what you need to collect, based on the benchmarks you have chosen, the next step is to determine how to collect the data.

Collection Techniques

You can collect data for your benchmarking exercise in a number of different ways. Often, your methodology will depend on the type of benchmarking that you are doing and the required kind of data.

First, if you collect either financial or volume-related data the best ways to record information is in a spreadsheet.

You can develop your spreadsheet so you record exactly the kinds of information you require for your comparison in the structure and format you need. Using a spreadsheet usually means entering information into the spreadsheet either directly from the source information or by adjusting the source information.

Whether you plan a broad-based benchmarking exercise or a peer-to-peer exercise, keep in mind that everyone's interpretation and definition of the data can be different, so you need to be clear and concise about what you need when you deal with others and provide definitions for those who will help you. When you use information from a broad-based benchmarking report, review the definitions to understand what is included or excluded from the specific benchmarking result. If in doubt, ask.

Broad-Based Benchmarking

For broad-based benchmarking, you collect only your own information rather than getting information from others, then compare your results with other published benchmarking data.

When you collect your information, you need to use the same approach and criteria that was used for the broad-based benchmarking information. Sometimes the benchmarking reports will provide enough information about collection methods. Where this information is not provided, seek the original benchmarking submission form that was used to compile the benchmarking data and use it as a guideline. Usually, these forms provide direction on the kinds of information to exclude and to include.

These forms can also be used as a basis for your own peer-based benchmarking activities, giving you an idea of the kind of information to collect and what to tell the people filling in the form.

Internal benchmarking

Internal benchmarking is usually used when you're able to compare between portfolios. If your organization is large enough to enable this, internal benchmarking is a useful tool to compare results between management and technical resources.

In this case, you should have access to consistent information for the comparison between the portfolios because the information should be contained within the same system or reporting mechanism. If that's not the case, steps should be taken to ensure that all information is consistent, so you can easily compare in the future.

If information is not contained in the same system or reporting mechanism, which might be the case with more decentralized departments or international portfolios, the collection process can involve reviewing and assessing the information and data that is available for the other portfolios or departments and converting it to the format and structure that you are using for your own. Alternately, you can provide spreadsheets and/or forms for your colleagues to fill in.

Peer-to-Peer Benchmarking

Peer-to-peer benchmarking requires the most preparation and the best tools to ensure that you're collecting the information you need in a way that you can accurately compare.

Even with the best tools, you will probably need to adjust some information or question your peers to clarify or verify information that's been provided. In some cases, your peers might not have access to information in the way you need it for an accurate comparison. In this case, you might need to you might need to exclude that specific information from the overall results.

Collection Tools

You can use a number of tools to collect the data you need for benchmarking. You can use a combination of tools, depending on the nature of the benchmarking in order to capture the full range of information.

Spreadsheets

A spreadsheet is a primary tool for collecting data for benchmarking because it enables easy analysis after the information is collected.

By setting up a spreadsheet with the exact information and data you're comparing and asking others to enter their information into the spreadsheet, you can make analysis much easier, and the data is much more likely to be in the consistent structure and format that you need to do comparisons.

Your spreadsheet software has many features that make this comparison even easier. For instance, you can use these features in your spreadsheet:

➡ **Tips** – you can add tips to cells so when the cursor hovers over the cell, the tip provides information about what to enter into that cell.

➡ **Drop-down** – you can set cells so they provide a drop-down menu selection. If you have a set type of information that you're looking for, you can ensure that it's entered correctly.

➡ **Data validation** – for every cell, you can set up the spreadsheet to validate the data that has been entered. For instance, if you've asked for a number between one and 100, such as a percentage, the cell can validate that the number is in fact between one and 100, and the software will advise the user to re-enter the number if it does not fall within the defined range.

➡ **Formulas** – you can allow users to enter data in one cell that is then automatically converted or adjusted in another cell of the spreadsheet. For instance, ask users to enter their office area in square feet and then use formulas in the spreadsheet to convert every cost item that they enter into the cost per square foot. You can also let them select metric or imperial measurements, so you can convert them consistently in the background.

➡ **Protection** – you can protect all the cells except for the ones that you want the user to enter data into. This means they can only enter data in the cells that you choose, and they will be unable to change formulas or other text information.

➡ **Worksheets** – your spreadsheet can have several separate worksheets, with tabs to access them at the bottom. Using this feature, you can have data grouped together and entered into separate worksheets. For instance, one worksheet could contain all financial data, another one could be set up for volume data, and perhaps another one could include staffing and/or practices-related data that you could capture in a Microsoft Excel spreadsheet.

By ensuring that your users enter data only into the cells that you choose and that the data entry is validated, you can more easily manipulate the data and combine it into meaningful information upon which you can perform mathematical operations and other analysis.

Forms

Forms are also a useful way to collect data, and these have been the traditional approach in the past, particularly for some of the larger broad-based benchmarking exercises.

However, electronic collection has become very easy, so paper-based forms should be your last resort.

While spreadsheets (which can be considered forms) are better for collecting data-type information, other types of forms can be useful for collecting other types of information, including comments and other text or checklist responses.

You can create a form using spreadsheet or word processing software, specialized form-based software, or Adobe Acrobat. If you use Adobe Acrobat or even MS-Word, your form can include radio buttons and checkboxes, drop-down selections, comment sections, and similar kinds of information. In addition, you can use Adobe Acrobat to distribute the empty form, receive the filled-in form electronically, and then have Adobe Acrobat combine the data for you in a way that you can download. You can then use a spreadsheet for analysis.

Interviews

Sometimes, the kinds of data and information you collect in the spreadsheet or form is insufficient, particularly when you're trying to determine other group's practices.

Include a formal interview process along with any data-type information that you collect from participants. Compile an interview form with specific, pointed questions and ensure that you include space to record interviewee's responses. Interviews can provide additional data that is not captured in the more formal data collection tools. Before you start interviewing, have a very good idea of the kind of information you're trying to get from the participants and how you will use it in your benchmarking exercise.

If you conduct interviews after the participants have submitted their data, you can use the interview as an opportunity to review the submission to clear up inconsistencies, confirm information, and get more context, which will help you with the analysis. The interview can also allow you to gain additional insight and nuances related to the information that you're capturing.

After you start analyzing the benchmarking results, be prepared to go back to the participants with more questions or for clarification.

Analyzing Benchmarking Results

By its nature, benchmarking includes a great deal of data from a variety of sources and organizations.

Having good tools to collect and manage the information as well as to validate and adjust it is important. Because universal definitions or approaches to documenting and tracking information are seldom available, it's important to validate that information is accurate and comparable to information from other sources.

Tools

For analyzing data, databases and Excel spreadsheets are the best tools available. In fact, a database is seldom necessary unless you are doing extremely broad-based benchmarking with a great deal of input.

The example provided in the section above shows you how you can use both the typical spreadsheet format and the pivot table feature of Microsoft Excel.

The keys to using Excel are to designate data consistently and to use the ordinary column and row structure with representative headings.

Even in a simple spreadsheet, you have a number of useful functions available. These functions include filtering information in a list, as shown below to limit the data to what is needed for your current analysis.

	A	B	C	D	
1	Organi ⌄	Amount ⌄	PSF Amoun ⌄	Primary Desc ⌄	Secondary
2	Org1	15(	Sort A to Z		Equip Ma
3	Org1	16(			Building
4	Org1	20-	Sort Z to A		Ser. Contr
5	Org1	50!	Sort by Color ▶		CONTRAC
6	Org1				Delivery
7	Org1		Clear Filter From 'Primary Desc'		Travel Ex
8	Org1		Filter by Color ▶		Members
9	Org1				INTERDEF
10	Org1		Text Filters ▶		PLANT M/
11	Org1		☑ (Select All)		COURSE F
12	Org1		☑ Bio-Med		Supplies
13	Org1		☑ Plant Maintenance		Rental/Le
14	Org1		☑ Plant Operation		Minor Eq
15	Org1	- 1!	☑ Plant Operation - Utilities		RECOVER
16	Org1	- 1(			OTHER RE
17	Org1				GROUP LI
18	Org1				OTHER EN
19	Org1				W.C.B. EX
20	Org1				HOODIP/
21	Org1				EI EMPLO
22	Org1		OK Cancel		EMPLOYEI
23	Org1				GRP LIFE
24	Org1	2,665	0.002551	Plant Maintenance	DENTAL-E

You could also include calculated cells that facilitate even more analysis, such as converting total costs into cost per square foot, which is a more valid comparison between organizations.

For example, participating groups provide accounting information that is then converted automatically to a cost per square foot within the spreadsheet for each line item (See 'PSF Amount' column in the next graphic). This information could be used to easily calculate totals and do comparisons on specific functions.

	A	B	C	D	E
1	Organizat	Amount	PSF Amount	Primary Desc	Secondary Desc
2	Org1	156,164	0.149529	Plant Maintenance	Equip Maintenance – External
3	Org1	160,878	0.154044	Plant Maintenance	Building Maintenance - Expense
4	Org1	204,897	0.196192	Plant Maintenance	Ser. Contract - Building Service Eq
5	Org1	509,282	0.487646	Plant Maintenance	CONTRACTED SERVICES
6	Org1	165	0.000158	Plant Maintenance	Delivery & Courier
7	Org1	290	0.000277	Plant Maintenance	Travel Expense - Staff General
8	Org1	474	0.000454	Plant Maintenance	Membership Fees
9	Org1	788	0.000755	Plant Maintenance	INTERDEPARTMENTAL CHARGES
10	Org1	1,689	0.001617	Plant Maintenance	PLANT MAINTENANCE EQUIPMENT
11	Org1	2,398	0.002296	Plant Maintenance	COURSE REG FEES AND MATERIALS
12	Org1	3,322	0.003181	Plant Maintenance	Supplies - Printing, Stationery & (
13	Org1	3,358	0.003215	Plant Maintenance	Rental/Lease of Equipment
14	Org1	8,769	0.008397	Plant Maintenance	Minor Equipment Purchases

You can also create graphs of all types directly from Excel spreadsheet data. This functionality gives you complete control over all aspects of the visual representation as well as the data included in the graph. Visual representation of your data is much more powerful than simply quoting numbers because the comparisons that you make are immediately apparent. In addition, when you change the information, your graph is updated automatically.

Pivot Tables and Pivot Charts

One of the most useful tools in Microsoft Excel is the pivot table and chart feature. This 'cross tabulation' feature uses your Excel spreadsheet to enable you to make a variety of numerical comparisons, including averages, sums, total number of entries, and even identifying the highest or lowest of the entries.

Pivot tables enable you to filter, sort, tabulate on any column heading and to make these kinds of changes on the fly.

The pivot chart feature enables you to turn data into a graphical representation. You can locate the pivot table and pivot chart features in Excel by clicking **Insert > Pivot Table**

The following graphic shows a very simple pivot table that cross tabulates functions in a row for each staff member in the department against the time each of those individuals spends on each of those functions. Using a calculated field in the spreadsheet, the Sum of Time column shows the time as a percentage of the total time for the department.

	A	B
1	**Row Labels** ▾	**Sum of Time**
2	Finance & Budget	20%
3	Lease Admin	3%
4	Locksmithing	5%
5	Manage Services	8%
6	Minor Moves (no construction)	6%
7	Other (new hires)	2%
8	Projects (with Construction)	21%
9	Purchasing	3%
10	Strategic	20%
11	Tenant Services	13%
12	Travel Services	1%
13	**Grand Total**	**100%**

The pie chart below uses the same information and shows it graphically.

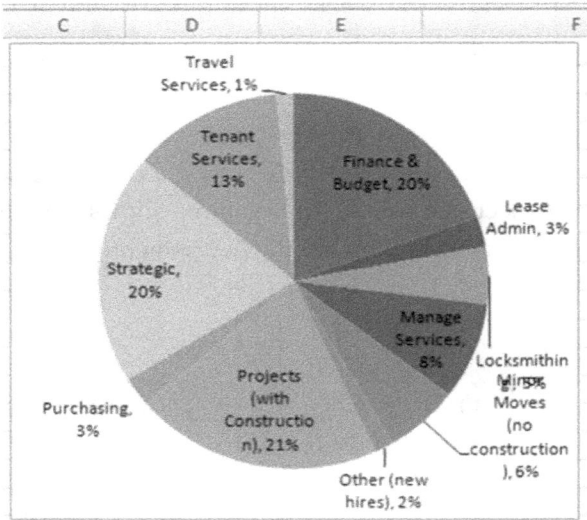

The calculations as well as what is cross tabulated can be changed on the fly with a drag and drop interface, which enables you to analyze and compare a broad range of factors with ease.

Validating

After you've collected your benchmarking data and during the analysis process, it's important to validate the information.

You can use the analysis tools described previously as part of the validation process. First, if you've collected detailed information, you can compile it into summary format and send it back to the participating organizations so they can confirm the totals. If you provide a form or a spreadsheet to participants for data collection, you can also include validation tools within the spreadsheet.

For instance, if you ask for component information on things like costs or volumes, you can include a field that automatically calculates the total for the participants, so they can compare it against their total. Or you can ask the participants to enter a total and then later, using your analytical tools, you can compare the total they entered with the calculated total based on the individual information they provided.

Another aspect of the analysis is to look at the details and see if there are outliers in the data. For instance, if an organization's result is well above or below the average, you should investigate the source data and validate it with the organization. This provides an excellent opportunity to determine whether or not there are some specific issues or practices that can account for the difference in the number. This clarification might yield either an insight that can help your benchmarking exercise or lead you to identify an area that requires adjustment in order to effectively compare between different organizations. Sometimes you have to exclude the results for the specific organization from your analysis if you can't reconcile the differences.

As an example, after collecting organizational chart information, it was compiled and a common function assigned to each of the titles. After this task was complete, the compiled information for each organization was provided back to the participants so they could validate that the assigned function correctly represented each position's responsibilities.

While it's not always possible to go back to the organization for confirmation, you should do it whenever there's clearly an issue with the information you've been provided.

Making Adjustments

Sometimes adjustments are necessary because of differences between organizations included in your benchmarking.

While the old adage of not comparing apples to oranges is true, when you start to do detailed benchmarking, you also have to be careful not to compare Macintosh apples to Golden Delicious apples. While on the surface, they're both apples, they are actually different. Sometimes, the differences aren't obvious from the outside, for instance, two red apples can have very different characteristics after you bite into them.

The same is true for services and organizations. For instance, two organizations that appear to be very similar (such as two insurance companies) might have different operating hours, different standards, different types of clients (institutional versus retail), etc., which all impact costs.

As an example, one of the most common adjustments for energy conservation and 'greening is made when comparing energy costs and/or energy consumption information between buildings in different geographic areas. In this case, you have to adjust for a common utility rate cost (if comparing cost) and adjust for the degree days (a measure of weather impact on energy consumption) for those locations in order to normalize the results. For instance, comparing consumption of utilities in a cold climate versus a warmer climate requires adjustment.

Even buildings in cities that you would assume to have similar weather might, in fact, have different weather or different weather for the particular year that you are comparing. Factoring in the degree days enables you to adjust results based on actual weather impacts, so you are comparing your efficiency, not the weather impacts.

Other factors also have to be accounted for. When you're looking at production costs between factories of widely varying ages, the differences might have less to do with operational practices and more to do with the efficiency of the production equipment (which may also be driven by how much lifecycle replacement is performed). These differences are why your adjustments need to be made in the context of the comparisons you're doing or use these differences as an explanation of how you need to make changes to your practices.

Similarly, comparisons between large and small organizations will not be valid unless you find a way of making adjustments in any specific benchmark data that might be impacted by the size differences. In some cases, you may not be able to find a valid adjustment, so you will either not be able to make comparisons or will have to make them in context.

Even factors, such as minimum wage, can play a part in cost comparisons for services, particularly those services with labor rates at or just above minimum wage. Where possible, you should try to find the typical or average wage rates in the geographic areas or for the specific services if you're doing this kind of comparison. Even if you do not adjust the results based on local conditions, you may be able to use the local conditions to explain differences caused by factors that might be outside your control. However, you still should look for other, more controllable, factors.

Sometimes, comparisons are too difficult to do effectively on a detailed, numerical basis. However, you can look at the practices, frequencies, and even the related tasks to see what practices you can use or change.

Your Benchmarking Plan – Making Adjustments

Use this table to identify the factors you might need to use for adjustment purposes. The factors drive the questions to ask or information to collect when doing benchmarking.

Benchmark	Factors That Impact Results	Your Situation	Factors to Adjust For

Notes

_____

_____

_____

_____

_____

_____

_____

_____

_____

_____

_____

_____

_____

_____

_____

_____

_____

_____

Understanding the Numbers

Since a key element of benchmarking is comparing numbers, it's important to understand how benchmarking numbers are represented and how to interpret them.

This awareness includes knowledge concerning common statistical definitions as well as the practical implications of the following terms.

Average/Mean

The terms 'average' and 'mean' refer to the same thing. They represent the sum of all values divided by the total number of values. The sample below shows the average cost per square foot of four different buildings. In this sample, the actual cost per square foot is added up to a total. Because there are four separate buildings, this total is then divided by four to arrive at the average or mean value.

While the averages are a useful tool for comparing one organization or activity against all others, you have to be aware of the limitations of the average. For example, it doesn't tell you anything about the distribution of the results. You could have three relatively low numbers and one high number that could arrive at the same average as for four numbers that are close together. When doing analysis, going beyond the average and looking at the distribution can be useful to provide more context.

The average or mean is found by dividing the sum of the results by the number of results. In the example below, the average is $2.32 by dividing $9.26 by 4.

Cost PSF	Results
$1.87	1
$2.12	1
$2.25	1
$3.02	1
$9.26	4

Weighted Average

A slightly better comparative for benchmarking data that relates to different buildings is the weighted-average. In the example below, we've added the total area of each of the buildings involved in this benchmarking exercise along with the cost per square foot. You'll note that the size range considerably from 10,000 sq.ft. all the way up to 100,000 sq.ft.

The weighted average considers the difference in size relative to the cost per square foot and puts a higher emphasis on the larger organization. So, in this case, the weighted-average average is lower than the simple average calculated in the previous section. The weighted average provides a more accurate representation. In any case, it is still critical that you also look at the individual results to understand the distribution and take that into account during analysis.

In a broad-based benchmarking exercise, you won't have the distribution available to you for review. However, the nature of the broad-based results, with many buildings included, should give you a much better representation as an average than a small sample size like the one shown would.

When doing internal or peer-to-peer benchmarking with a relatively small number of buildings, you should always do a comparison on an individual basis, which will show you the complete distribution of results.

In this example, using the same Cost PSF as the previous table, the weighted average is found by dividing the total cost by the total sq.ft, which results in $2.11. That is less than the non-weighted average of $2.32.

Cost PSF	Sq.Ft.	Total Cost
$1.87	75,000	$140,250
$2.12	100,000	$212,000
$2.25	50,000	$112,500
$3.02	10,000	$30,200
$9.26	235,000	$494,950

Median

The median is simply the middle number in the list of numbers. It means that half the results are above and half the results are below the median. When benchmarking, the median is not a useful analytical tool if you have the actual detailed data available to you.

In addition, as explained with the average, the median can sometimes be deceptive because of the distribution of results. You'll notice that in the two tables below the results for the median are the same. However, the average is very different. This discrepancy is simply because of how the two different results are calculated and illustrates the difficulty in using either the average or the median as an absolute comparison.

Cost PSF	
$2.05	
$2.11	
$2.12	
$2.13	
$2.25	Median
$2.67	
$3.36	
$3.67	
$3.81	
$2.69	Average

Cost PSF	
$1.87	
$1.96	
$2.12	
$2.13	
$2.25	Median
$2.34	
$2.36	
$2.57	
$2.61	
$2.13	Average

Percentile

The percentile is an extension of the median calculation that allows better refinement of the number of results that are higher or lower than any given point. As you can see, the 50 percentile is also the median which is also the 2nd quartile. The first quartile means 25% of the results are below that result and 75% are above. The third quartile means 75% of the results are below and 25% are above.

The percentile is useful when you compare your organization against peers in broad-based benchmarking because it gives you a more refined indication of where your results sit relative to the other participants. However, it's less useful in internal or peer-to-peer benchmarking where you have a much smaller number of samples that you can compare directly.

Cost PSF		Percentile
$1.87		100%
$1.96		88%
$2.12	3rd Quartile	75%
$2.13		63%
$2.25	2nd Quartile (Median)	50%
$2.34		38%
$2.36	1st Quartile	25%
$2.57		13%
$2.61		0%
$2.13	Average	

Assessing Your Performance

After you've collected, adjusted, and analyzed your benchmarking information, the next step is to assess your performance against the benchmark.

While you might have done this during the analyzing stage, assessing performance against the benchmark usually just provides you with numerical information rather than strategic information.

While the initial analysis might provide information on your performance relative to others and might even provide you with information on practices that the leading organizations use to achieve their performance, you need to properly assess this information in the context of your organization's goals to decide on the next steps.

What does Better mean?

Of course, the first thing to decide is what 'better' truly means. Having lower costs doesn't necessarily mean better. In fact, lower costs might result in poor services that negatively impact core business activities or reflect a lack of maintenance and lifecycle replacement that degrades your organization's assets over time and introduces risks that the organization doesn't want to take.

In addition, higher volume or shorter time frames for various processes might sound better and could potentially result in lower costs, but you need to assess other impacts, such as quality of the outputs and potential risks.

So, defining what better truly means and whether or not you want to strive to meet the benchmark results of other organizations is an important part of your benchmarking exercise.

If you've done a strategic benchmarking exercise, instead of simply comparing numerical information, you'll now have information you can use in combination with your own organizations goals and requirements to determine what, if anything, you should do to change your results.

Are the gaps real?

If you've collected all the information for your benchmarking exercise with a process that ensures consistent information and you've validated and adjusted as needed, you should be able to say with confidence that the gaps in performance are real. Otherwise, you might be comparing your results with results from other organizations that are not actually comparable. In such a case, you might then chase improvements or changes that either will not materially affect your results or will have a negative impact on your organization's core business.

In addition, if you see a high degree of variability in the results across the participating organizations, the true comparison might be difficult to determine. Look closely at the very high or very low results to ensure that they are not anomalies before you select them as results you want to achieve. Additionally, while other organizations might have results that are worse than your measurements, such as a higher cost, lower volume or longer timelines, they might achieve better results overall through lower rework, higher quality, better consistency, and lower risk.

Why does the gap exist?

Because you've collected as much relevant information as possible on practices in addition to the numerical comparisons through your strategic benchmarking exercise, you're now in a good position to determine which of those practices you should emulate, rather than simply looking at the gap between your results and others.

This is where the real value of the benchmarking exercise reveals itself. While the first step is to identify where the gaps exist, the next step is to determine why those gaps exist and apply the practices you need to close the gaps.

Example

One organization had operating costs that were high compared to most of the other participants on a cost per square foot basis. Information on practices and follow-up interviews suggested that the level of scheduled maintenance activities was relatively consistent between these organizations and further analysis of wage rates and in-house versus subcontract work activity showed that these were also relatively consistent. In looking at other practices, two differences stood out. First, the number of separate unionized trade classifications for their predominately in-house resources directly correlated to cost. The organizations with the smallest number of trade classifications had the lowest costs while the organizations with the largest number of trade classifications had the highest cost. Second, the organizational structure of the lowest cost organization was different from all the others and represented what appeared to be a more effective way to coordinate work activity and make the most efficient use of staff resources. The lower number of trade classifications also enabled more efficient management of work activity because it placed fewer limits on individual staff who could perform any given work and eliminated the possibility that certain staff members would be idle because there wasn't enough work at any given time for their specific trade classification.

Deciding on the action to take

The changes you make based on the benchmarking exercise are not always clear from simply comparing benchmarking results.

Based on your assessment of the gaps, you determine whether a particular gap is real based on your review of the practices. Then, based on your assessment of the underlying reasons for the gap, you review what changes to make, keeping in mind any substantial differences between your organization and the leading organizations in your study.

Finally, you consider the impact that the changes might have on your own organization and your ability to make those changes, since practices that work for others might not be relevant for your specific situation.

Rather than simply move ahead with changes, some changes should be carefully reviewed and assessed to determine both the positive and negative impact they might have. Sometimes there are unintended consequences that you won't want to face.

For instance, in a previous example about unionized trade classifications, the number of trade classifications was identified as a practice that should be changed to improve results. However, your portfolio might be large enough that your larger number of trade classifications works better for your situation, and a change will result in higher, not lower costs. Even if you don't end up implementing the change, you can be confident you have looked at the options.

If you identify many potential changes, use a matrix to compare the potential benefits for each change with the level of effort for each change, which can include implementation costs, time, effort, or risks involved with making those changes. Start with the high-benefit, low-effort options and work your way through the initiatives.

Your Benchmarking Plan – Your Gaps

Questions

What core business activities do you potentially impact and what can you benchmark to assess whether you are achieving the required results. Understanding the most important business activities you impact will help identify the items to benchmark and the additional information you need

1. Where are your gaps?

2. What can explain the gap?

3. Is the gap under your control?

4. If the gap is under your control, what can you do about it?

Notes

Section 2 – Conducting Benchmarking

Conducting a benchmarking exercise can be time-consuming, yet rewarding.

The principles discussed in Section 1 – Foundations of Benchmarking are critical to your success, whether you do a broad-based exercise or focus on one single area to compare.

This Section outlines specific processes and approaches that you can use to conduct your benchmarking exercise. These methods support the principles from Section 1 as well as provide specifics on how to effectively conduct the three different types of benchmarking: broad-based, peer-to-peer, and internal.

General Benchmarking Process

The general benchmarking process provides an overview of the steps you should take to conduct your benchmarking exercise using the principles in Section 1 – Foundations of Benchmarking.

In addition, more information and details are provided further below to help you implement the various steps of your benchmarking exercise with the different types of benchmarking: broad-based, peer-to-peer, and internal.

Conducting a benchmarking assessment of your operations involves many different components. It's important not to simply conduct a superficial assessment that might lead you towards initiatives that don't match your company's strategic objectives. Implementing leading practices just because someone else is or making changes because the metrics you compare indicate you should might be counterproductive.

This process is designed to step through the process and target problem areas, then identify solutions and changes you can implement that will get better results.

These 10 steps represent the overall process you should use to conduct your benchmarking exercise. They are also grouped and summarized into five main stages as illustrated in this graphic:

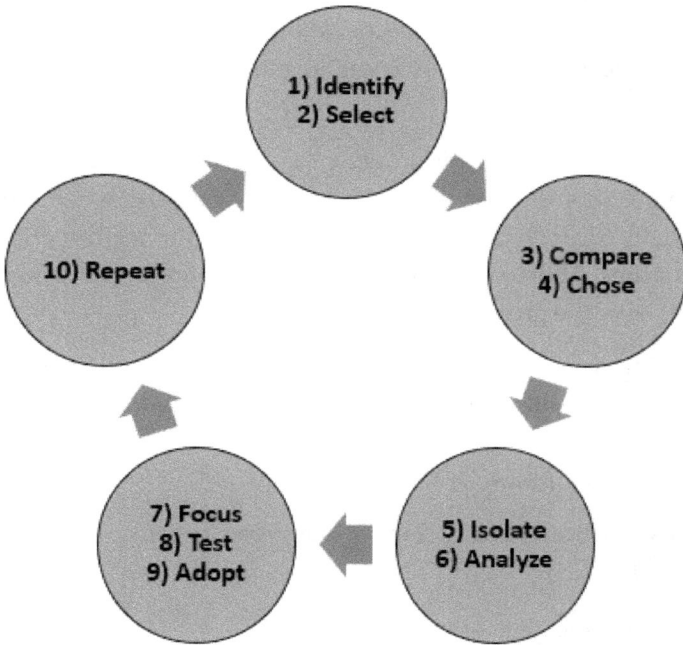

Now we will review each of the 10 steps.

1   **Identify** Critical Success Areas

Before you begin, you need to know what is important to your organization. You support your core business and the activities and processes you do will have an impact. Establish the activities and processes with the biggest impact that you have influence over.

Your critical success areas will be those that support the goals and objectives of your organization, which will often be different from other organizations. It is important to note that while some goals and objectives are fundamental, others are very specific to your own organization's approach to their core business.

Because your critical success areas support your organization's core business, these areas are where you should focus your attention initially in your benchmarking activities. They will typically be areas where improvements will have the greatest impact.

Having said this, don't focus just on these areas. There are often many things within your operations that don't appear to be critical; however, they can ultimately have an impact on the success of those critical items.

These critical success factors for your organization could include:

➡ Revenue generation
➡ Cost containment
➡ Customer service
➡ Your organization's image
➡ Reliability
➡ Service response

2   Select Areas to Improve

After you have identified the critical success areas, select the ones you can improve. At first, choose just a couple to target and make sure they are high-impact areas that you can make changes to. For the first round, don't waste your time on things you will have a hard time changing or influencing.

3   **Compare Results** Using Broad-Based Benchmarks

Use broad-based benchmarking information to compare results in the area you have selected. This information includes industry benchmarking reports from both within and outside your industry sources, studies and reports, colleagues, and internal comparisons.

4   **Choose Results** that are not Superior

Carefully assess the results and choose the benchmarked results where your performance is either equal to or below the benchmarks. Leave the ones that perform better for later, although you will be able to find improvements in those areas too.

Start with large-gap, high-priority items. Then, after you have addressed the large gap, high priority items, work your way through others with less opportunity.

Use a matrix like the diagram below and plot each of the benchmarks as high or low in either gap or priority.

Focus your attention on the benchmarks in the high gap, high priority section first then move to the other sections once you have addressed the high priority ones.

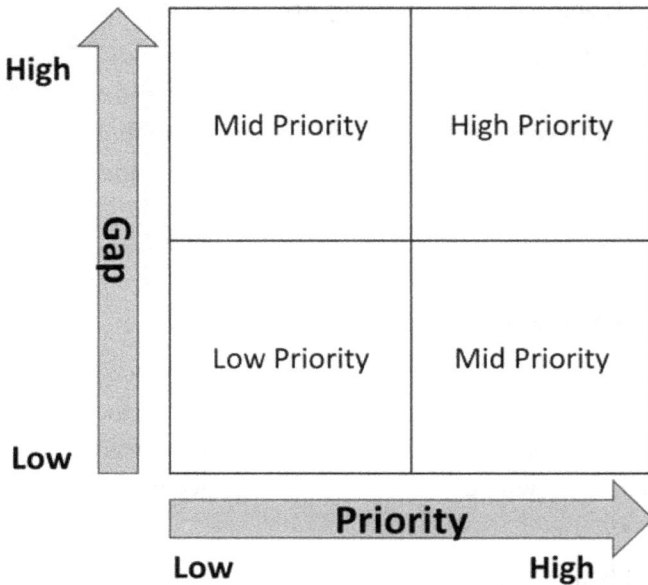

A 2x2 matrix. Vertical axis labeled "Gap" with "High" at top and "Low" at bottom. Horizontal axis labeled "Priority" with "Low" at left and "High" at right. Top-left: Mid Priority. Top-right: High Priority. Bottom-left: Low Priority. Bottom-right: Mid Priority.

5   Isolate Supporting Processes, Resources, And Systems

For each of the areas where the results aren't better than the benchmarks, dig deep to identify the processes, resources (including staff, supplies, subcontractors, etc.), and systems that are used or required to get results. These elements would all support the areas you are focusing on and should be things you can influence or change. Ask yourself the following questions to help direct your queries.

➡ What drives the results you measured?
➡ What do you have control over?

6   Analyze Process, Resource, And System For

Impacts

One by one, analyze each of the processes, resources, and systems to see where there are bottlenecks, performance problems, and other issues that prevent results. Compare what you do to what others do, ask your staff and suppliers for their input and suggestions and investigate all possibilities.

Here are some things for you to consider:

➡ Look at a granular level
➡ Assess practices
➡ Identify bottlenecks
➡ What impacts your results?
➡ Ask "Why"?

7   Focus On Problems

The problem areas will become evident and you can then focus on those areas, gathering more information and going into more detail as required by doing the following:

➡ Establish high-value issues
➡ Learn more about them
➡ Get input and feedback
➡ Leverage internal expertise

8   Test Your Practices Against Leading Practices

Collect information, understand what is happening, and seek out other direct benchmarking information to compare your practices with. Your comparisons shouldn't be simple number comparisons, it should include how you are organized, the type of systems you have in place, training you provide, and procedures you employ.

➡ What you do and don't do
➡ What others do

9   **Adopt** Leading Practices And Change Existing Practices

When you have identified leading practices that are better than yours, develop a plan to adopt them in your organization and create an implementation strategy.

➡ Learn from leading practices (not best practices)
➡ Plan and implement change
➡ Reinforce and validate your changes (follow-up)

10   **Repeat** for other Areas

Now that you have found and fixed one critical success area, start again and improve the next critical success area that you identified in Step 1.

➡ Start over with the next critical success area

If you chose a single area, be sure to also include practices and comparisons that impact that specific area, as described in Section 1, so you can more readily differentiate results you should emulate from results that you shouldn't.

Broad-Based Benchmarking

For most managers, broad-based benchmarking involves using published benchmarking data from associations or other organizations that conduct these studies.

Benchmarking Studies

The first step is to purchase the benchmarking results. These are commonly available in paper format in a report or as a database. Some are also available on-line.

The database can be a more effective means of conducting broad-based benchmarking because it gives you more options for categorizing and analyzing than what is provided in paper-based documents.

Review available Benchmarks

With the benchmarking results in hand, you can look through the results and decide which of the benchmarking results you want to start your comparison with.

Refer to Step 1 and Step 2 (Identify & Select) in the general benchmarking process to help you decide which result you should start with. You may choose one or a group of benchmarking results, but you should start with the one that can provide you with the best impact.

Gather your Information

The next step is to compile your own information to compare with the published benchmarking results and to chose which ones are superior to your own, following Step 3 and Step 4 (Compare & Chose).

To chose which results are superior to yours, you need to understand the basis of the published benchmarking results, which will allow you to compile your own data to match the data represented in the benchmarking study.

The report itself will provide some information, such as definitions for various benchmarking results and some description of the elements (i.e. what is included in certain cost components), but you might need to find the original survey document to understand how the information was captured in the first place.

With these definitions and explanations, you can source the information within your own organization in a way that is compatible and compile it so you can properly compare your information with the published benchmarking results.

Analyze the results to determine where your results sit relative to the published benchmarking results, following steps 5 and 6 (Isolate & Analyze) from the general benchmarking process. You can use the analysis tools discussed in Section 1 - Foundations.

Act on the Results

The next step is to assess the practices to find what you can implement to improve your results. Follow steps 7 and 8 (Focus and Test) to identify changes needed and then step 9 to Adopt the changes.

With a broad-based benchmarking exercise, testing is something you might be able to do for some benchmarking results, but not for others. When the benchmark is simpler, such as with staffing levels or other elements that you can combine to discover what you can do differently, the benchmarking results might point you in the right direction.

> **Example:**
> For staffing levels, the benchmarks on staffing for specific-sized operations were sufficient. Yet when they were cross-referenced with the volume benchmarks, it demonstrated that the resourcing level was much lower than the initial benchmark showed and additional resources were in fact warranted.

For other elements, such as maintenance costs, there are too many variables to definitively know what your changes should be. However, the benchmarking exercise can point you in specific directions by looking at several of the related benchmarks, for instance, in-house or out-sourced percentage, application of computerized systems, staffing levels, etc. This exercise can be the starting point for a more detailed internal or peer-to-peer benchmarking study.

The Next Step

In most cases, the reason for doing the broad-based benchmarking in the first place is to identify those areas where a more detailed benchmarking exercise is warranted. Otherwise, you might spend time doing benchmarking that doesn't provide you with the ability to make improvements.

Based on the results of the benchmarking, you can initiate additional benchmarking, moving to the next items on your priority list. Or, you can move to the next level and conduct a peer-to-peer benchmarking exercise to help identify what others are doing to achieve better results.

Peer-to-Peer Benchmarking

Peer-to-peer benchmarking is done instead of or following broad-based benchmarking because the peer-to-peer exercise enables you to dig deeper into practices and approaches that others are doing to get better results.

This type of benchmarking can be done on a wide range of factors. Because it requires much more intensive data collection and analysis on a broader range of elements for each individual item you're looking at, the process is simpler if you focus on a small number of items or a single item .

Getting Peer involvement

The biggest challenge with peer-to-peer benchmarking is gaining the involvement and cooperation of your peers. Having a network of your peers already in place can be valuable.

The advantage to your peers is they also get the benchmarking information, so they can use it internally as well. This benefit should be your biggest sales pitch to them and their organization to get their participation.

Depending on what information you're trying to benchmark, confidentiality is sometimes a stumbling block. If you can't overcome the confidentiality block with the peers you want to benchmark with, you can engage a third party consultant to conduct the benchmarking exercise in a way that does not reveal confidential information or even the names of the participating companies.

To gain their involvement, you should provide them with the following information:

> A benchmarking plan which identifies what information you're collecting

> How you will maintain confidentiality between the participants

> The level of effort that may be required on their part (which may include a site visit or telephone interview, for instance)

> What they will receive back for their involvement in your benchmarking exercise.

While the peers you contact might be comfortable working with you on a peer-to-peer benchmarking exercise, their senior management might be more resistant, feeling their competitive and confidential information will be revealed. Some organizations don't participate in broad-based benchmarking exercises for the same reason, even when confidentiality processes are in place. If resistance is the case, you will need to mount a sales pitch to help your peers convince their senior management.

Sometimes, by modifying or limiting the sensitive information that's collected, you can get participation from others. Do this only if the benchmarking will still achieve your objective of discovering practices that you can use to improve results.

Example:

In a benchmarking exercise, only compiled financial information (i.e. summary cost for maintenance, not the breakdown) is included

in the report for confidentiality reasons even
though the breakdown information was used
for some analysis.

As well, each participant receives tables and
graphs that show individual results compared
to others, but the other participant's names
are not revealed.

When you invite peers to participate, include organizations
that are similar to your own. Doing so will make valid
comparisons easier, and it might even make the collection
process easier. However, it is often useful to include other
organizations that are not in the same industry but have
some similarities. Because you are digging deeper than
broad-based benchmarking, the practices and approaches
used by organizations to achieve their results is as important
as the actual results. Sometimes you can learn more from
non-related organizations than from your own direct peer
organizations.

Example

In an office space allocation benchmarking
exercise for a government organization, non-
government organizations with primarily
administrative/corporate buildings were
included in the benchmarking exercise. While
government and non-government
organizations can be very different, the use of
the buildings was similar. The comparison
provided valuable insight into how the non-

government organizations were handling
their space allocation policies.

Decide what to benchmark

Unlike broad-based benchmarking exercises, you are
essentially working with a clean slate because you can choose
to benchmark almost anything that you can get information
about. As indicated above, it's useful to start with the broad-
based benchmarking exercise so you can pinpoint areas
where your results might be weaker than others.

To determine what to benchmark, follow Step 1 and 2
(Identify and Select) to establish your priority list and then
have initial discussions with the peer organizations to verify
that the information you will need for these benchmarking
items will be reasonably available to you. If it isn't, either
select new peers to include in the exercise or re-evaluate the
information that you are trying to benchmark.

Collect and Compare

You need to collect the necessary benchmarking information
from the peer groups and then use step 3 (Compare) to
compare your results with the others.

As described in Section 1 – Fundamentals of Benchmarking,
several methods are available to you for collecting
information. Because this isn't a broad-based benchmarking
exercise, the volume of information collected will be
relatively minor, so the more sophisticated methods aren't
required.

However, when you collect financial information or other numbers, using a standardized Microsoft Excel spreadsheet, which you provide to each peer organization will improve consistency and make compilation and analysis much easier.

This method makes data collection easier for participants because they know the format in which you need the data; however, this method can also make collection more difficult for them because they might need to translate their data into your format. An alternative, which is more time intensive for you and typically means more follow-up, is for them to provide you with information in the format and structure they have. You then must rework it into a common format. This approach is easy to do with staffing positions, for instance, but much more challenging for financial information.

Example

Participants provided their existing organizational charts with their staffing information instead of being asked to fill in a form. Each position was entered in a spreadsheet with a corresponding common position title, which enabled a more relevant comparison between organizations with different titles and organizational structures. Each participant then validated the assumptions and changes if necessary

You can also use an Adobe form to collect information, particularly for non-financial information. It can be an easy approach, which is more fully described in Section 1.

For some benchmarking, all you need is a site visit and an interview form with some capture of simple numerical information, particularly when you are looking for practices.

After you have collected all the information, the first priority is to check it for consistency and validate the information. If there any anomalies or questions you need to ask about information, you can go back to your peers to validate and verify it. This step is important to ensure that you have the correct information for effective comparison. In some cases, based on the information you receive, you might need to adjust their information. For instance, when you consider operating costs in office buildings, the hours of operation impact costs, so if comparable buildings have much longer or shorter operating hours, you will need to either adjust some of the costs, such as those related to security and or HVAC, or take this fact into account during analysis.

Analyze the Results

After you complete the collection and verification process, you can start to compare results. Keep in mind that this comparison will provide you with guidance on areas to examine in more detail. Even if another organization's result is less favorable than yours, you might find practices or approaches that they are using that can benefit you.

Based on your comparison, you would then follow Step 4 (Choose). Begin your analysis, particularly if you've chosen to start your benchmarking on a wider variety of measurements.

Identify Practices to Adopt

After you've chosen results that are not superior, move on to Step 5 (Isolate) and start to identify the practices and approaches that your peer uses to achieve results. For instance, if the time it takes for peers to respond to a work order requests is much shorter than yours, you would assess the processes, resources, and tools that they use to achieve those results. Remember to adjust data for the situation, such as rural or urban locations.

If you haven't already asked for additional information about these processes, resources, and tools, this is the stage where you can revisit them and investigate further. This is also the step where you determine whether there are factors in either your organization or your peer's organization that would limit your ability to make changes or adopt the practices. It's important to understand what is possible and what isn't before you move further. Keep in mind that you shouldn't simply abandon a potential change because it might be more difficult for you to implement. Rather, you should understand the limitations and avoid spending time on factors that simply cannot be changed. Just be sure that you have thoroughly examined whether the limitation is real or imagined.

Next, based on the information from the previous step, you will use Steps 6, 7 and 8 (Analyze, Focus, and Test) to examine each potential change and issue against your current practices and approaches to determine which ones you can adopt. This analysis might provide you with a prioritized list of things, ranging from simple and cheap to complex and expensive, that you may well want to adopt. Based on the results achieved by your peer, try to quantify the improvement you can achieve and any resulting benefits. These could be quality, risk, or financial benefits to your organization, depending on your core business.

Implement changes

Finally, in Step 9 (Adopt), you either implement the changes that you've identified, or you build a business case to gain approval for any initiatives that you can't implement internally. Some changes will be simple changes that you can adopt immediately. Others might require a strategic plan for implementation to ensure they are successful.

After you've started to implement the first round of changes, you can repeat the process to benchmark the next item on your priority list.

Internal Benchmarking

Internal benchmarking is quite different from peer-to-peer benchmarking yet can also provide reliable and useful results in a large portfolio. Internal benchmarking relies on a multi-office portfolio where services or functions are managed or serviced by different individuals or companies.

The intent with internal benchmarking is to compare the effectiveness, processes, and approaches used by different individuals across your portfolio. Even if most of your service delivery uses a centralized, regimented approach, you might still find areas where performance is higher because of specific practices that are being done in other places.

The process you take will either conform to the steps described previously or follow a modified version of the process because you're completing only internal comparisons.

Similar to peer-to-peer benchmarking, it's useful to start with a broad-based benchmarking that helps you pinpoint areas you should focus on, which would encompass the first four steps.

Then, when you've determined which benchmarks are worth reviewing in more detail internally, repeat the compare and choose process to establish which of those internal benchmarks demonstrate a clear leader within your portfolio.

You could bypass the broad-based benchmarking stage and start comparing results directly within your portfolio. If you have easily available information that you already track, measure, and report, this way is a very effective approach your internal benchmarking exercise. For instance, if you have systems that provide you with reports on each team's performance, you can identify differences in results.

With this kind of information, you can quickly identify and select areas where there is a clear leader and then start the process to analyze why they had better results than the rest of your portfolio. You can then try to emulate those reasons in the rest of the portfolio.

You can follow the same logic for virtually anything where you have measurements. For different teams or different regions, your benchmarking analysis might reveal differences that are driving higher costs.

Remember that even with internal benchmarking, you might need to validate information and make adjustments to ensure you are making appropriate comparisons. Even services, teams, departments, regions, or organizations that seem equivalent might have differences that need to be accounted for.

Internal benchmarking can also require you to interview various participants. For instance, you might need to interview the managers who are responsible for certain regions or the staff who are directly involved in any of those regional teams or services.

Internal benchmarking can be particularly useful in discovering differences that result from the individuals themselves, including their background and training. For instance, if you compare energy consumption between factories and then analyze the high-performing and low-performing factories, you might discover that the operator's skill level at the low-performing site indicates that the operator hasn't been fine tuning the system's operation, which means the factory has a less efficient system. In comparison, the high-performing site has a highly skilled, highly experienced technician who is able to fine-tune the system. This kind of information provides an opportunity to identify increased training requirements or to change how you operate so your most highly skilled operator visits other buildings periodically to help those operators.

Develop your process and your communications in a way that gives individuals assurance that your internal benchmarking process is meant to help everybody by sharing techniques and ideas with everyone, not to focus on the actual results. However, when the changes are made, be sure to measure the improvements to verify that the changes were worthwhile and to congratulate your staff on a job well done.

Internal benchmarking should be a continuous process. If you have systems and measurements in place to provide you with ongoing information, you should be constantly reviewing that information and identifying areas where improvements can be made.

Section 3 – Implementing Change

Sometimes, the actual benchmarking process is the easiest part.

Making changes as a result of your benchmarking process is the most important reason for benchmarking; however, if you are unable to implement the changes, your efforts might be wasted.

Preparing for Change

If you are benchmarking, hopefully, it's to find things you need to improve or change, so be prepared to implement changes before you even begin.

You might be tempted to take your benchmarking results and simply implement change immediately. Unfortunately, every change, no matter how small, impacts your staff or your suppliers and without sufficient planning and communication, you're less likely to succeed at getting the improvement in results that you expect.

Start at the Beginning

Preparing for change means starting the change process at the same time that you start your benchmarking exercise.

Everyone involved in or impacted by your benchmarking exercise should be aware of what you're doing and why you're doing it. In particular, your senior management should be aware of your initiative, and expect changes to be recommended to them for approval. Don't be shy to identify things that need improvement – identifying issues and making changes is a more positive statement on your leadership than trying to sell the status-quo as the best it can get.

Prepare your organization for the possible outcome, which might include organization changes, business cases for new systems, or developing/implementing new processes or activities. These things take resources, so be ready to develop a strong business case and sell your change.

Making changes takes effort. Plans aren't worth anything unless you implement them, so be proactive and push for changes and take action. With change, you will get results, get attention, and get ahead.

Prioritize

Depending on the results, focus your plan on only one thing at a time. After you have successfully made changes, move to another area, if you found more than one.

How you prioritize will depend in part on your own specific organization's needs. The impacts you need to assess when prioritizing your initiatives include the following considerations:

Improvement

This is a quantitative assessment, where possible, in the results and is based on the changes you want to make. For instance, for energy, improvement could relate to consumption savings and related costs. For process changes, improvement might be reduced handling of paperwork, with a corresponding savings in labour or labour that can be applied to more important issues. You can also assess improvement in relation to quality where relevant, as long as you can put it in a quantifiable form.

Costs

Costs refer to the cost to implement the change and perhaps the ongoing costs of the initiative. You can use a lifecycle approach to the costs of your new initiative relative to the status quo. Costs are not always direct, so be sure to identify all the resources, for instance, that have to be involved, even if the resource doesn't directly result in additional funds spent. For instance, implementing a maintenance management system will cost in real funds and resources, while a major change in your processes for responding to maintenance work orders or delivering specific services might only require existing internal resources to work on it.

Time

Time is a factor when it comes to both costs and improvements. Something that can be realized quickly will usually take precedence over initiatives that won't see results for over a year unless the financial business case is compelling. For example, a process change that you decide to implement based on practices from other organizations might be something you can do immediately, while implementing new software or designing/tendering/installing new equipment can be done only over many months. Take time into account when you prioritize, particularly because some quick results can provide you with the credibility within your organization to tackle longer term initiatives.

Risks

The risk relative to costs and the improvement you expect must be assessed. Some results will be clear; others are less concrete, and the risk is that your initiative doesn't truly result in an improvement. This is another case where the lower-risk initiatives should be tackled first. Even if they are lower value, successfully implementing them will help you develop credibility and a track record that enables you to move on to higher-risk changes.

The other part of risk is the impact to your organization. For instance, initiatives to reduce your department's costs might negatively impact your organization's core business. This risk can't be ignored and might even be the real reason your results are not favorable compared to benchmarks, reflecting a conscious decision to reduce risk rather than reduce costs, for instance.

Selection Process

Chose the initiatives based on the previous factors. Use a matrix table like the ones we discussed before and use the factors to decide, assessing each element as high or low. Start with the improvement/cost analysis on a grid and select the most likely initiatives. Then take those initiatives and do a risk/time comparison to narrow down the initiatives.

This process should be a guide only. Other factors will influence your selection process, including core business requirements.

Be aware that you won't always find changes that will improve results or lower costs, depending on your own organization's priorities and issues. These considerations might prevent you from achieving results that others have achieved; however, you should always review the opportunities and investigate options.

Selling your Initiative

While you might have to sell your initiatives to get needed funding, resources, or approval, you should start selling even before you start your benchmarking exercise. Your sales job shouldn't just include those who have the power to approve, but those who you will need to help implement change – your own staff and colleagues.

To sell your initiative means identifying the reasons you are conducting your benchmarking exercise and preparing everyone for the potential outcomes. By getting buy-in at the beginning, you are more likely to get buy-in for the initiatives that you put forward to make changes based on the benchmarking results.

As mentioned, include your staff and colleagues in your sales pitch. It's important to present the benchmarking initiative in a non-threatening way, highlighting the opportunities related to change and reassuring everyone that suggested improvements and initiatives, which might result from the benchmarking, don't mean they aren't already doing a good job. Position the benchmarking exercise as a learning opportunity, and ensure that your staff and colleagues are involved in the process from the beginning.

You can bring your supervisor and others who you need approval from on board by getting them excited about the potential outcomes and preparing them for your inevitable request for funding, resources, or other changes. Then keep them in the loop during the benchmarking process. With your encouragement, they can become excited about the improvements. By demonstrating to them with evidence from your exercise as you work through the comparisons, they will be ready to accept the final analysis and see the value of moving forward with the initiative.

Along with the selling process, you need to be aware of the roadblocks you may have both to participation internally and to the ultimate changes you recommend.

This includes the standard change management issues and objections:

Disagreement With Your Findings And Recommendations

If you've done your due diligence during your benchmarking exercise, you should be able to demonstrate the validity of your findings and how the recommendations were developed. Try to differentiate between recommendations based on definitive facts and where you made assumptions.

If you involve people who might be involved in subsequent changes during your benchmarking process, you're much more likely to have their buy-in when the recommendations are established.

Resistance To Change

Resistance to change is a classic problem with all change. The best approach to disarm this resistance is to start early with your communications and discussions and gradually demonstrate not only the benefits of the process to the organization, but also the benefits to the individuals themselves. Some of the resistance is based in fear over losing control, losing their job, having to do things differently or learn something different, or even being unable to adapt to the new changes. When you encounter resistance, identify the actual resistance and focus on dealing with it first.

Not-Invented-Here Syndrome

This resistance usually comes from people who are trying to protect their turf or feel diminished in the role because changes or solutions are coming from somewhere else. This attitude can be particularly difficult if you did internal benchmarking and are attempting to implement processes or approaches that originate from a colleague. If you recognize this attitude in your staff, deal with them one-on-one to assure them that their skills and abilities are just as important as ever, and encourage them to help with the implementation and perhaps even improve it.

It's The Way We've Always Done It

When staff are asked to change what they do or how they do it, particularly if they've been in the position for a long time, the situation can be very difficult. Some staff might hang on to the old way simply because it's comfortable and they know it well. In addition, they might be skeptical that the changes you recommend will actually be better, considering the effort they will have to make to change their ways or learn new processes.

One way to deal with this resistance is to sit down and do a detailed walk-through of the current process and your recommended changes. At each step, challenge the individual to provide input and feedback about what will and will not work. This procedure will help gain buy-in from the individual and might also identify things you have not considered.

We Tried That Before (And It Didn't Work)

It may be true that some of your recommendations have been tried in the past; however, circumstances change. In addition, the previous staffing, funding, processes, and culture might not have been able to properly support the initiative when it was originally implemented. One way to deal with this issue is to ask the individuals to identify what precisely did not work when it was tried before and what can be done differently this time to make this initiative successful. Again, it's a strategy of drawing in the detractors, listening to their opinions, and benefiting from their experience while gradually getting their buy-in.

Your Benchmarking Plan – Dealing With Objections

Questions

1. What are the objections your boss, colleagues, or staff might raise about the changes you are recommending?

2. How can you overcome those objections?

Notes

_____

_____

_____

_____

_____

_____

_____

_____

_____

_____

_____

_____

_____

Strategy

After you decide which initiatives to pursue, develop your strategy for the implementing the changes, whether they are relatively simple changes that you can implement on your own or changes that require approval for funding, resources, and time.

For simple changes, you can be use a simple approach that outlines your strategic plan and implementation steps in a few pages. Don't underestimate the need to develop your strategy and be sure you include communications with everyone involved and your expectations for improvement. Simply implementing changes because others have achieved success with the techniques doesn't mean you will automatically achieve those benefits yourself. Your staff and colleagues should be involved in the process to ensure changes are implemented in a way that works for your particular organization.

For larger or more complex changes, break the changes into manageable parts and implement those parts in stages, both minimizing the resources requirement and maximizing your chances of success. Show results from one change or part of the change, and then gradually implement others to achieve the maximum benefit.

The Business Case

If you need to get approval for the changes, develop a compelling business case that is based on the benchmark results and estimates of improvements in quality, reduction in risk, or reduction in costs based on the changes you're recommending. You can use the benchmark results as a basis for demonstrating the improvements in your business case. However, in some cases, you might have to do additional analysis to be sure of the impact on your results.

If you've done a rigorous benchmarking process with effective adjustments, validation, and analysis, you will be able to prove what you are proposing in your business case, which adds to your credibility when you ask for resources. Referring to other organizations that have already done what you want to implement will also help your cause by establishing its validity as a viable solution. If your change will impact another department's productivity or costs, work with that department to quantify the possible impact and use that in your business case.

Whenever possible, quantify the improvement in your business case in a way that will impact whoever is approving your business case. For instance, if you are pitching your business case to the Executives or the finance department and you believe you can reduce costs by 3% with your change, multiply the cost reduction percentage by the total cost and present the figure. If it's a recurring cost, multiply it by 3 or 5 years to demonstrate the real magnitude of the value.

If your change will mitigate risk instead of specifically reducing costs, look at the result of the risk and establish a cost around that risk or failure. Use good comparative information and a concrete example to make it more meaningful.

Implementation

Your Action plan should have two parts: the initiatives that you've decided to proceed with, which you established previously, and the implementation.

The implementation is, arguably, the most important of the two parts. Without implementation that gives you success, the initiative won't have delivered results. Keep in mind that the implementation plan might call for further analysis and study to verify that you will get the results you expect. This further work could be a pilot, deeper benchmarking, or testing of some kind.

What are the roadblocks?

A sure way to fail in your implementation is to encounter a roadblock that you can't overcome. So, before you implement, consider all the potential issues to implementation, including the ones you documented earlier as objections.

Roadblocks can be a variety of things, from resources, time, and funding to approvals, technical issues, roadblocks in other departments, and lack of buy-in (and therefore active support) from your staff.

How can you overcome the roadblocks?

When you've identified the potential roadblocks, you should establish a way to overcome them. For instance, if buy-in from your staff to a process change is expected, develop a communication plan with all the necessary stakeholders.

Demonstrate improvements, address concerns they have about their jobs, work with the Union to get their buy-in and seek champions within your staff who are respected by others to help sell the initiative.

In some cases, when you find a roadblock you should address it immediately. Speak with your superior to get advice. Go directly to the appropriate department head to discuss the issue, develop a specific and focused plan to address the roadblock, and solve it in advance.

What resources do you need?

Your action plan will likely depend on having the necessary resources: money, staff, and cooperation from other departments or suppliers. By knowing what you need, you can start the process to get approval or buy-in for the resources. For example, if a process change needs a software change to existing company systems, you will need resources from the IT department. While the software might not be a direct cost to you, if the IT department is too busy or doesn't see your project as a priority, you won't get the resources you need and your initiative won't get done.

What are the Timelines?

Depending on the initiative, you might be able to implement your changes quickly or they will take a lot of time to finish. Knowing your timelines and ensuring you have the capacity to complete your changes are important. Beyond that, setting realistic, yet firm, completion dates are necessary to ensure everyone involved has a target to achieve. Otherwise, your initiative may drag.

What are the main steps to implement your plan?

At this point, you can start planning the actual activities that your initiative requires. You can use a project management approach (and related software) for large initiatives or a simple table or spreadsheet with space for updates, milestones and dependencies to help you stay on-track for smaller, simple initiatives.

Your Benchmarking Plan – Implementation

Questions

Answer these key questions to help you develop your implementation plan:

What are the roadblocks?

How can you overcome the roadblocks?

What resources do you need?

What are the timelines?

What are the main steps to implement your plan?

Notes

About the Author

Michel Theriault is Principal of *Success Fuel for Managers*, a training & consulting firm that provides strategic and management support to help managers assess, analyze, develop, and implement initiatives to get better results.

Other books by the Author

Quick Guides for Managers (Series):

Thinking Into The Corners
Published 2014

Write To Influence
Published 2012

Win More Business - Write Better Proposals
Published March, 2010

Managing Facilities & Real Estate
Published December 2010

Contact Information

Please feel free to connect with the author.

Blog:	www.successfuelformanagers.com
Twitter:	www.twitter.com/micheltheriault
LinkedIn:	www.linkedin.com/in/micheltheriault
E-mail:	michel@successfuelformanagers.com